How To Make Money Doing Junk Removal

Your Step by Step Guide to Navigating This Lucrative Business

Dave Merton

Legal Disclaimer

This book does not offer legal or accounting advice. You should retain the services of a professional for these types of services.

Copyright © 2014 by David M. Merton Jr.

All rights reserved, including the right of reproduction in whole or in part in any form. No part of this book may be reproduced, scanned or distributed in any printed or electronic format with permission.

How To Make Money Doing Junk Removal   by Dave Merton

ISBN-13:   978-1494951269
ISBN-10:   1494951266

Acknowledgements

There are just too many people to thank for this project so I'll keep the list really small:

Thank you to fellow author Jourdan Cameron who helped me through a few of the ins and outs of self publishing.

Thank you dually to Steven Silver of the Yankee Pennysaver for not only providing a great advertising platform for when I was engaged in the junk removal business, but for also being supportive on this project and not even hesitating when asked if I could mention the Yankee Pennysaver as a resource.

Thank you lastly to George Repasky who let me leave mountains of junk on his front lawn along with my 'FREE' sign. I know how much you used to hate that!

Introduction

Folks, please be aware that this is my first book ever. I have read hundreds of them and have *considered* writing hundreds, but this is my very first actual attempt. Please go easy on me with respect to reviews; I have done my best and after a monstrous amount of time I believe that I have put together a very instructive and valuable how to guide for anyone who would like to give this business a shot.

My goal was to make the outline of the book as logical as possible; however, some things are naturally repeated throughout as they are important for more than one reason. My feeling is that if something important is stated more than one then it is better than not stating it at all.

Each chapter is 'self contained' so that it can be picked up and read at a later time, but still give you the entire thrust of the chapter without you needing to flip back and forth to other sections. I also have tried my best to reference other sections or chapters that may contain related material in the event that you would like to read more about the related topics without needing to re-read the book from cover to cover.

With these few thoughts in mind I hope that you proceed with an open mind and put faith in yourself if you decide to give this business a fair try. You won't be disappointed, believe me.

Contents

1	Why Do Junk Removal?	9
2	10 Ways to Make Money	15
3	Equipment	33
4	Vehicles	47
5	Advertising	57
6	Pickups	65
7	Disposal – Getting Rid Of Stuff	71
8	Estimating Jobs	93
9	Handling Difficult Questions	105
10	10 Commandments	109
11	What I would Do Differently	127
12	Funny Stories	131
	Resources	139
	About the Author	143

Chapter 1 - Why Do Junk Removal?

Depending on the area where you live, and on how the economy is doing, you may be able to make some extra money part time, or even full time, with *very little* initial investment. The hourly rate of pay can also be extremely high. You are really going to love that part. If you play your cards right, netting $60 - $80 an hour is completely doable. I've made over $100/hr several times. It's very possible, and I'm going to walk you through as much of it as I can.

Note: The economy plays an important role because when there is a booming economy, people tend to move more often. When people move, they usually have to get rid of a pile of junk. This just adds to the need for a junk removal service. That being said, in any economy, there is always the need for junk removal. I will also go over with you *other strategies* that you can employ *in addition to advertising* that will keep you busy.

Overview

The reason why this business can be so lucrative is that people in America do a few things more frequently and with more impunity than in other nations:

- They *acquire* lots and lots of junk.
- The *hold onto* this junk.
- They inevitably must *part company* with this junk.

These are three by-products of the 'American Dream'. If you don't think that people in America collect a lot of junk, please do the following: Make a list of 5 people that you know; who each have a two car garage. Find out how many of them are still able to pull both cars into the garage. Chances are it will be one or less. Also, when they say that they cannot park both cars inside, ask them why. It's usually because the garage turns into the primo junk-storage-area for

most homes. In chatting with these folks, this may be a good segue into how you are going to be doing junk removal. ☺

I did junk removal for years. When I was actively doing it, I actually was able to either earn cash and/or increase my net worth *ten* different ways! We'll be discussing them in more detail in Chapter 2.

If you are wondering just how feasible it would be for you to start your own junk removal business; please consider the following list of pros and cons.

Pros

- <u>No training necessary!</u> Can you carry stuff from a house to a vehicle?

- <u>No college!</u> You do not need any kind of a degree to cart away junk.

- <u>No licenses!</u> There are no licenses necessary (that I am aware of) for the purposes of junk removal.

- <u>No uniforms!</u> You really don't need uniforms. My 'uniform' was usually a t-shirt and jeans.

You really only need a phone and a truck.

On top of that, Americans are generally wasteful. (Not all, but most.) If you are planning on operating this business in the US, well then, congratulations! Because the US has lots and lots of junk!

If you are in New England, then it is even better, because New England has been referred to as "The Nation's Attic". There is junk and more junk.

Cons

The image factor can be a con for some people.

Allow me to elaborate:

Okay, let's just suppose that you are a single male in his mid to upper thirties. (Yeah, we'll just suppose...) You happen to be at a friend's wedding and you are dancing with a very delightful young lady whom you've never met before today. The very delightful young woman happens to ask you, "So, what do you do for work?" It's usually better to be able to say that you are either a Nuclear Physicist, Software Consultant, or even a Cab Driver than to say "I'm in the Junk Removal business." All they hear is "Sanford and Son". Believe me, this is an unrecoverable situation. Don't try saying "Personal Property Relocation Specialist" either, all they will hear is "Sanford and Son" as well as "Con Artist". Not only is this one unrecoverable, but she'll make jokes about you to all of her friends. BTW, just as an aside, I've also learned that you never tell someone, that you just met at a wedding, whom you are dancing with, and who is rather delightful, that you are the Ice Cream Man. (This just shouldn't need to be explained.) If the delightfulness factor is sort of not there, then go for it. It will protect you.

You owe me one.

The "Junk Removal 1-2-3"

Before we get going and delve into specific areas of junk removal I would like to mention a few important philosophies. They are super important to your profitability and cannot be over-stated. If you can understand the spirit behind these following three statements, then you will be able to extract the most amount of profit, with the least amount of pain, from your future junk jobs. That should always be your goal in really any business.

1. Get junk jobs: quickly, easily and cheaply.

Dave Merton

    2. Do junk jobs: quickly, easily and cheaply. (cheaply for you)
    3. Unload junk: quickly, easily and cheaply.

These are the three keys that almost all the other information in this book will revolve around. These are also the first three of my "10 Commandments of Junk Removal". All of these commandments will be mentioned in the different chapters of this book as appropriate and will then be reviewed, with examples, in Chapter 10.

Whenever a key idea or "Commandment" is first mentioned it will be highlighted like the examples directly below, followed by a brief explanation:

Commandment # 1

Acquire Junk Jobs *quickly*, *easily* and *cheaply*!

Explanation: The acquisition of junk jobs needs to be as quick and easy and inexpensive as possible. When you first get started you will need to advertise, most likely in a newspaper, if they still have one where you live. This will bring you immediate calls which are both quick and easy. Finding the best advertising vehicle in this regard is important, because price matters. Not necessarily the total cost of the ad, or the cost divided by distribution, etc, but really it is the total cost from the ad divided by how many calls and/or jobs that you get from it. We will discuss this in much more detail later, but just a quick example: If an ad costs you $100 and you get 3 jobs then it would have cost you $33 per job. That is really high. My best newspaper ad back in 2003/2004 was so good that it ended up costing me only $6 for each new job. That is a very low customer acquisition cost. If you are right in between, even at $20 per job, that isn't really too bad. You can still make tons of cash. We will also cover different ways to increase traffic (new calls/jobs) w/o doing any paper advertising or internet advertising.

Commandment # 2

Do Junk Jobs _quickly_ and _easily_!

Explanation: The picking up of junk needs to happen quickly, easily and cheaply. This means that you need to be organized and smart. If you need a second person, get someone well in advance who is dependable. Two people work quicker than one person and on bigger jobs why do all the work yourself when you can pay an hourly helper? I would rather pay someone $20/hr for 3 hours and walk away with $340 for 3 hours of work rather than make the whole $400 but have to spend the entire 6 hours myself. Your hourly rate for the first scenario is in excess of $100/hour (which you can do all the time in junk removal) while it is only $67 an hour doing it the second way. Plus a helper is more fun. If you are good with advertising and scheduling and organizing, you might even have time for a second good size job if you have the helper. The sky is really the limit. I mean, until the people in your area run out of junk, which will never, ever happen…

Commandment # 3

Unload Junk _quickly_, _easily_ and _cheaply_!

Explanation: The unloading (discarding/reselling) of junk needs to be an intelligent blending of receiving decent compensation, if any, as well as speedily getting rid of the items. This means that if you can actually sell an item right now for a few dollars, or get rid of it for free, you still might be better off than holding on to an item in the hopes of making a few extra dollars later. Each case is different and we will discuss this with examples in later chapters.

Chapter 2 - Ten Ways To Make Money

You may be surprised to learn of all the ways that you can earn extra money *on top of* the initial cost of charging your customers to remove their junk. You get paid to take it away and then sometimes other people pay you real money to take the stuff away from you. It's like being a middle man with no real product. Lots of variety too. This whole aspect of free enterprise in places like the U.S. is really a wonderful thing. Where else could you possibly do this so easily? And where else do people acquire junk so readily and regularly? It's like a competition.

1st Way - Initial Removal Costs

This will be the largest portion of your earnings, by far. This is your first and foremost income stream in this business.

The profit on my average job was around $180. That's after advertising and paying to get rid of the stuff, so soup to nuts net profit. You may do even better. You will have many jobs for a lot less than that, and some that will be several hundred or even a few thousand per job. Your bread and butter though will be the nice juicy $300 to $500 jobs where you are basically removing a few clunky pieces of furniture and then some smaller odd items. Those jobs are the best because people expect to pay through the nose (so why disappoint them?) and the items should be easy enough to pay a small fee and dump them quickly. (Commandment # 3)

Note: The prospect of reselling things that you remove from houses should never cloud or affect your judgment to the point where you are lowering your prices to get the stuff. That would be crazy. Remember, they called you because they never want to see this stuff again.

You should always charge accordingly; however it still is true is true that 'One man's junk is another man's riches''. ☺

Dave Merton

2nd Way – Flea Markets

Flea markets can be a great way to unload junk on other folks. The good news is that not only are you not having to pay to get rid of stuff, but people are actually paying you to walk away with it! People will buy almost anything. Plus, this puts the items back into circulation. Just maybe they will be calling you in five years to come get the same stuff! ☺ Talk about true recycling!

There are some pros and cons:

Pros

- You can make a ton of cash.
- You can network.
- Anything that sells doesn't have to be dumped or reloaded.

Cons

- You usually have to get up very early in the morning. ☹
- You need to bring a helper, who'll have to get up early. ☹
- It costs a few bucks.
- It's usually on the weekend.

The flea market that I used to go to was the Elephant's Trunk, in New Milford, CT. It was two miles from my home and four miles from where I parked my trucks. It is one of the most well attended flea markets in Connecticut. You may or may not have access to a flea market like that.

I had to pay forty bucks to get in, and I averaged three hundred in profit, plus the savings of not having to pay to get rid of the stuff I sold, each of the fours time that I went. This was after paying the forty bucks and paying my helper. You need a helper because it's nicer, you need to be able to speak (haggle) with more than one consumer at the same time, and you'll inevitably need to use the can, even if you are as tough as a Bavarian.

3rd Way - eBay

Just about everyone alive has heard about eBay:

www.ebay.com

If you've ever sold anything on eBay, then you know just how lucrative it can be. You can sell anything from comic books to jewelry to power tools.

When it comes to junk removal you will want to take advantage of this area of potential. Also, the things that you can sell on eBay (from your junk removal business) do not have to be collectible things like baseball cards or comic books or old dolls. They certainly can be, but more often than not they will be things that you would also possibly sell at a tag sale, like a smaller pair of used stereo speakers or even bulkier items like an Electrolux vacuum cleaner.

I can remember selling a used Electrolux on eBay. It was *old*. But when it comes to an Electrolux, most people realize that 'old' really means 'vintage'. Even an older unit can still out-perform a typical upright vacuum that you buy brand new at the store. People searching for an old Electrolux on eBay realize this. They keep their value, like an old Mercedes. This one that I sold went for around $130.00, plus the buyer had to pay the shipping on it.

I was giddy standing in line at the Post Office when I was shipping the vacuum. It was the easiest $130.00 ever. Plus, my less than expert packaging job (slight irregular bulges) was actually quite fun to work on.

When I was handing the 'packed vac' over to the mail clerk I was also amused at her slight discomfort. She had to measure it every which was to see if it was within 'allowable measurements'. It was, just barely. I would have hit it with a sledge hammer to make it the right size at that point if it was over the allowable limit.

Dave Merton

The experience almost felt like I was doing something illegal. I made $130.00 as opposed to having to *pay* to get rid of this item. Actually, you can always find someone willing to take a running Electrolux off of your hands, but you get what I mean.

It only took me a few minutes to take a picture with my phone, and then put the vacuum on eBay. The hard part for me is waiting the seven days for the auction to finish.

I have a couple Electrolux canister units at my house. (If only I used them more often.)

Now, when it comes to eBay, there are actually a few smart ways that you can do this. There are three ways that I know of, but only two that I would personally recommend.

Here are the three ways:

1. Do it yourself- This is the most work, and the most cash.
2. Hire a trusted associate – This is actually my favored way.
3. Hire the services of an eBay seller company – I wouldn't do this.

Here are my descriptions of each item as well as my explanations of my statements immediately following each item:

Do it yourself

As mentioned above, this method is the most work, and the most cash. If you love selling on eBay and are familiar with the process, then you may want to stick to this method. It also helps if you live close to either a UPS drop off site or a Post Office.

Now, even if you do live close by a Post Office, that particular location may not always be there, so you need to think this over. Disappearing Post Office locations have really affected many

How To Make Money Doing Junk Removal

individuals who have earned the majority of their incomes via eBay sales.

Hire a trusted associate

The reason why this is actually my favored way is that it follows the principle of making the most money with the least effort.

If I can make $20.00 doing zero work, then to me that is infinitely better than making $30.00 - $40.00 that I had to kill myself for. Even if the $30.00 - $40.00 only took an hour or more, I would rather have the $20.00 by doing zero work. It's cleaner and much more profitable, time is money. The sooner you understand this concept the sooner you will be an unstoppable money machine, in any business.

Here is my formula for *finding* the right person to do this:

1. They must be someone who has already proven that they can *sell* on eBay.
2. They must be someone who has proven that they can *make money* on eBay. (This is *not* the same as item #1!)
3. They must be someone who has already proven that they can get the job done *quickly* on eBay. (No procrastinators)

Here is my formula for *compensating* the right person to do this:

1. They handle *all of the costs* for selling the items on eBay, *whether the item sells or not.*
2. They give me 20% (yup, that's it!) of the selling price.

Now, let me explain why I set this up like this. One of my associates, we'll call her Nina, was an avid eBay seller. She was going to sell a bunch of old toys and games that I acquired from a junk job. Actually, to make this even better, like the Holy Grail of junk removal, Nina was one of the folks that was helping me on the actual junk job. We put the games right into here minivan. I never had to pay to get rid of

19

these games, I never had to deal with them in any way whatsoever. I just had to cash the customer's check and grin.

Now, I would have never sold these items on eBay on my own, because it just would have taken me forever, and I was just not organized enough to take on the task of taking pictures of all these games with all the pieces, etc. It would have been too much for me, but not Nina. I would have tried to sell them at the flea market, and then got pennies, while the people buying them would have gone right to eBay with them. This is just reality.

Nina sold the games and toys. It took her a few weeks to unload them all. She told me that she spent the better part of a week checking al the games for parts and taking the pictures and putting it all on eBay, so she truly earned her money. When it was all said and done, Nina raked in over $900.00 total! I NEVER would have extracted that much from these games and toys, I was out doing junk jobs, construction jobs and I had to travel to Redwood City, California to go to a friend's wedding. This means that I made $180.00 for doing *nothing*!

Actually, it wasn't 'nothing', I was just using my head. Plus, Nina raked in a cool $720.00 less any eBay costs. Therefore it was a win/win.

Note: I would recommend using this exact ratio of 80/20. Don't get greedy. Make it completely worth it to your trusted associate, your Nina, and they will make it worth it to you.

Learn to network and think Win/Win.

Hire the services of an eBay seller company

I wouldn't do this. Whenever I investigated it I thought that the fees were high, considering that I was at *risk*.

Why? If the item didn't sell, I still would have had to pay! Can you see a slight flaw in that model? What would prevent them from auctioning off a useless item, starting with a ridiculously high bid price, and then running a losing auction? Nothing, I would still have to pay a fee. The model doesn't work.

My 80/20 no risk model is perfect, trust me. The trusted associate, the Nina, is 100% motivated, and when you make the 20% cut for doing nothing, you will be dropping off a lot more stuff to Nina for eBay.

That means that they are less incentivized to make a sale than my Nina was. In her case, the expenses were on her, not me, and I just received a percentage of the gross sales.

4th Way – Networking With Other People

Networking will both educate you and fill your pockets with extra cash that you never even would have known about, if not for networking.

The good news is that you will be networking with real people, honest people. You don't have to deal with Tony Soprano or Silvio Dante, I mean, unless you actually know real, honest people in real life, named Tony Soprano or Silvio Dante.

When I speak about networking with other people I am talking primarily in this section about networking with others who specialize in certain niche items, like antiques. You certainly can, and should, network with other types of people, like realtors.

To find folks who specialize in certain areas you need to initially be proactive, but after a while you will start hearing about other good people to network with through the grapevine. From one couple that owned an antique shop I also eventually met a woman who was a 'fabric queen' meaning that she dealt in high end fabric. Um, as a guy, I didn't even know that people of that type were in existence. Did I miss an episode of jeopardy or something? Through the antique couple I also was introduced to an auctioneer. So, as you can see, once you break into a group, it's like being at a party and very soon you get

to meet all the other players. But you really need to be proactive about finding the first few people in this process.

I recommend just stopping into an antique store and letting the owner know what you are doing. Let them know that you would be happy to bring them anything that might be an antique.

Any antique dealer will jump on this, since it is free merchandise. Normally the antique dealer gets 20% of the sale of one of your items as a commission, but I liked my antique couple so much that I gave them 30%.

You need to just ask the antique dealer to educate you as to what to be looking for. It is usually not what you might think. My antique guy took me around his shop immediately and gave me a very helpful lesson.

Now, this is a key point: My antique guy was willing to educate me. This knowledge transfer, even if brief, has the potential to make money for the both of us. I find that people that are both hones and also not greedy have no problem with sharing what they know with others.

The following week my antique guy came down to my storage unit and took a peek. I was surprised by what he took with him as opposed to what he left behind. Antiquing is not always intuitive. BTW, my antique guy only took three things from my storage. The first thing was a wine funnel. (Yeah, I never heard of those either.) The other two were a pair of old large wooden salad bowls.

Now, I would've tried to sell the bowls at a flea market for $10.00 a piece, but then after the annoying but inevitable negotiating process I would've eventually settled for $5.00 a piece. However, the networking paid off royally because my antique guy sold one of the two bowls for $300.00 at his shop the next day! I rec'd a check for 70% of that and the beautiful thing is that I didn't have to do anything. I mean, other than deposit the check.

Not every story is like that, of course.

Another person that I met was the 'Fabric Lady'. She dealt in high end fabric, hard to get fabric, etc. After I did a large job that had lots of old fabric and old linen sheets, etc she came to my storage unit and took a look. She made a small pile of folded fabric, maybe a foot or two high. It was a bunch of small pieces. (I would have thrown them out, or worse, paid to throw them out, or used them as exotic designer rags, because I didn't know any better.) Any way, 'Fabric Lady' said to me, "I'd like to offer you $250.00 for that little pile of fabric!". I immediately said, "And I would like you to do that!" After that she further advised me exactly how to unload the rest of my stuff (the linen sheets, etc) at the flea market. She was right on, I made a small fortune. But here is the key: Like my antique couple, 'Fabric Lady' educated me.

So here's the deal, if you are selling lots of fabric at a flea market, fold them into small piles and put them right on the ground on a large blue tarp. It works like a charm. People will buy old linen sheets like they are going out of style. (Oh, because they did actually go out of style...) They can be ripped, they can someone else's monogrammed initials on them, funky discolorations, etc. It doesn't matter, people will buy them anyway.

These are just two brief examples of how you can network with people right in the area in which you live or plan to do this business. Opportunities abound everywhere; you just need to think creatively.

5th Way – Free Classifieds

You can definitely make use of Craig's List, although I have not personally done this for junk removal. The reason why is that in my area we have a really good paper journal called the Bargain News. This periodical is paid for at the news stand and comes out every Thursday. It is free to place an ad, you just have to call on the phone. If you place an ad online it will cost you. It has everything in it from cars to comics to chainsaws.

Dave Merton

Did I mention the free part? Free as in free. It works too. I've sold cars, computers and other assorted junk through it, as well as bought a bunch of stuff through it, like both of my junk vehicles, the van and the box truck.

One of my favorite sales through the Bargain News was a pinball machine that I took out of a garage. The recycling center wanted me to pay them $30 to take the pinball machine. Can you believe that? A dishwasher is only $5, why would I pay $30? So I thought I'd try it out for a week in the Bargain News. As soon as it hit the news stand my phone started ringing. I had someone at my storage unit later that afternoon and they paid me $180 cash for the pinball machine. The gentlemen buying the unit said that he was going to have to fix it up a little bit and them make some money with it. I hope he did really well. This business is all about win/win. Why let the pinball get crushed and put in a dumpster, then to only wind up in a landfill? The pinball guy was happy. I was happy. I bet even the pinball machine was happy. Oh, the recycling center, sans $30 big ones, probably not happy.

I am a true fan of the Bargain News. Plus, I didn't have to heft the machine back into my truck to dump it, we just set it in the buyer's pickup truck and he drove away, off into the afternoon... Sigh...

Anyway, here are the heroes I was referring to:

www.bargainnews.com

See if there are any similar publications in your area.

6th *Way – Scrap Metal*

You can make money scrapping metal as opposed to simply recycling it. The folks that cart away your recycling are going to eventually get it to a scrap yard. Why not you? Make some money, help the environment. Help your financial environment while you are at it.

The metal has to be sorted by which type of metal (copper, brass, plutonium) and then also by which grade of metal, like cooper wire or roofing copper. If it is mixed they weigh it and pay you based on the lowest price of what is in it. BTW, they hate when it is mixed. Be nice, sort it.

You just need to find the closest scrap yard. It's not worth it if the scrap yard is several towns away. Usually there is at least one near you, because the demand is created by the amount of metal stuff available in your area. Look right in the yellow pages or go to:

www.google.com

...and type in:

scrap yards near 12345

... where 12345 is your zip code. The closest ones will come right up after the few mandatory ads.

If you want to get a really accurate idea of what the going prices are go to google and type in

scrap metal prices

To narrow the search parameters you will probably want to either add your state's initials or better yet your zip code after the search term like this:

scrap metal prices ct

scrap metal prices 06776

Look for a site that is laid out well and that is very good about updating to the latest prices.

Dave Merton

At the time of this writing, November 2013, these are some of the prices that are a reputable scrap yards web site:

#1 Bare Bright Wire	$2.85 /lb.
#1 Copper Tubing/Flashing	$2.60 /lb.
#2 Copper Tubing/Bus Bar	$2.40 /lb.
#3 Roofing Copper	$2.20 /lb.

That should give you a rough idea s to why you may want to apportion a small amount of room to accumulate some metals. The copper prices were actually a little higher than that recently, they fluctuate.

Check out the prices for aluminum:

Aluminum Siding	$0.52 /lb
Aluminum Grills	$0.48 /lb.
Aluminum Ladders	$0.45 /lb.
Aluminum Rims	$0.60 /lb.

Do you have any idea how much aluminum is out there? You will be taking it in all the time. Although it is much less valuable then copper, it is way more abundant in the junk removal business. Aluminum is in window frames, siding, barbecue grills*, etc. If you have any free storage space that is easy to get at but out of the way, then you can let it accumulate until you are ready to go for a trip to the scrap yard. That means maybe the side of the house or under the deck if you are married. If you are single it means the garage, the front lawn, kind of wherever.

* Note: Barbecue grills that have been unused for lengthy periods of time almost always have bee's nests in them, so be very careful. You would have figured this out the first time, but I just wanted to give you a heads up. They must love something about the barbecue architecture, because it sure isn't the lingering smell of burnt food.

How To Make Money Doing Junk Removal

Some items that you may want to scrap will require you to have to 'clean' them first. It's time consuming for pennies, so don't bother, just recycle that stuff.

What about steel? Don't bother scrapping it, compared to aluminum and stainless steel it is effectively worthless. I mean if you are going to the scrap yard anyway, maybe, but it just isn't worth it.

Check out these current prices:

Steel $0.06-0.10/lb.

Those prices are for a minimum of 500 lb, so unless you have like 5 miles of train tracks, it's not worth it. That's $120/ton. A ton! I wonder how much time that would take or how much gas. Don't deal in steel.

Note: Copper is copper and it looks like copper. It is either penny colored or green like the statue of Liberty. Steel and aluminum are impossible to distinguish to the untrained eye. Get yourself a small, powerful magnet to test if metal is steel or aluminum. Aluminum is not magnetic, steel is very magnetic.

Note, if you need a magnet in a hurry, and are fresh out of the, look on any refrigerator and there will be maybe 20 or more. It will not be the best, but it will hold you over until you procure a nicer one.

Stainless is sometimes magnetic, but you can tell stainless steel usually in comparison to aluminum. For a refresher, go through the kitchen and look at the pots and pans, they all say what they are made of. Do this when the wife is not home, or she will think you are nuts and make fun of you.

7th *Way – Tag Sales*

You can usually squeeze around $100 or more out of a correctly executed tag sale. You need to have 3 things:

Dave Merton

1. Good weather
2. Good traffic*
3. Good 'merchandise'   (business people term for 'junk')

* The traffic is based partly on location. Busy streets are best, with decent road side parking if not off street parking. You also need to consider a few well placed signs to steer folks in your direction. Don't forget to check out the funny story about when I forgot to take down a tag sale sign. It's near the end in the chapter X -*Stuff Happens – The Inevitable Humor in Junk Removal*.

8th Way – You Can Pay Helpers with Junk

One of my helpers wanted something from a job. I can't even remember what it was, some kind of fabric or something, who knows. We had an understanding that if a helper was interested in something that we could work something out where they could have it but that it meant that they would get less money for the job. It still worked out, she was happy as can be and I ended up paying her maybe $10 or $20 less. Big deal, it just means that I didn't have to deal with or pay for getting rid of whatever the thing was.

This only happened a few times, but the potential is really there. You just need to make sure of something very important. You need to make sure that the helper understands that they are to never ask you about something that they like in front of or anywhere near the customer. The reasons should be obvious but I will state them anyway:

1. If it is something of value and the customer hears that, they may decide to keep it.
2. They may want to then pay you less money because you took away less stuff. Silly, I know…

Example:

Soon-to-be-ex-helper:

How To Make Money Doing Junk Removal

"Hey boss, can I have this oil lamp? You won't even have to pay me for today."

Customer:
"Oh, I, um, meant to keep that item."

Me:
<doh!>

Then, after that, you might also get a litany of strange questions like: "So what do you do with all this stuff?" – Like it's gold all of a sudden. Although it might be tempting, avoid saying that you eat most of it.

So basically, even though most helpers are pretty smart, you really need to state to them the rule about never asking about something they like in front of the customer.

9th Way – You Get To Keep Stuff

This point may not seem like cash per se, but it really is not that different.

I can't tell you how many times I had wood to burn for myself and others or that I had something that I took in that I could use and that I would have had to go pay money for elsewhere.

If you happen to burn wood for heat, this can be an opportunity to score some free resources. The burnable wood can come in several forms:

1. Lumber – old/used 2x's, etc.
2. Brush Components – Twigs, sticks & branches (kindling).
3. Shipping Pallets – These are usually made from oak, so they are excellent for both kindling and larger burnable pieces. Carefully cut them up with a circular saw, if you try to pry them apart you will break your back.

Dave Merton

Note: There are several types of woods that you should never burn, due to the toxicity:

1. Plywood – The glue can be harmful.
2. Pressboard - The glue can be harmful.
3. Painted/Stained wood.
4. Pressure Treated Lumber.
5. Other – Any type of wood that has been chemically treated in any way.

Right now in my house, 10 years later, I can see a dining room table that I've kept, along with two small dressers, in the same room where I am typing away on the computer. There is also a large wall mirror that I like.

I'm still looking around and I see a basket, several books on the shelf and finally some packaging tape and a bunch of hand tools. (You can never have enough hand tools and you will take in more of them than you ever dreamed possible.)

In the next room I have these two really nice glass vases that I really like and that magically the cat has knocked over yet. Okay, as a guy, especially a bachelor, I never would have bought the vases, but you get what I mean.

10th Way – Trade

This might surprise you, but if people know what you do, they will actually be willing to barter with you.

Once, my van actually broke down on a job site. I was on the person's rear lawn so it was rather embarrassing. I contacted a former mechanic of mine, who had moved on to another business. He came out to the site. It was only a few miles from his house. He had figured out in 10 minutes that all I needed was a solenoid, which I bought and installed the next morning. The fellow wouldn't take my money. He said that

How To Make Money Doing Junk Removal

he would call me soon and he did. When he called, he just wanted me to get rid of an appliance. It was either a dishwasher or washing machine, I can't really remember. But either way, I stopped by his house, put it on the truck, and dropped it off at the recycling center, as I was headed there anyway.

What was my cost, aside from my time? Five dollars! Just imagine if I needed to get towed and then have a mechanic fix the problem. I would be looking at a huge bill, probably around $200 at least, and there really wasn't any good way to get a tow truck down on this lawn where I was without having to reseed a bunch of grass and probably have the customer lose it and strangle me. Five bucks was a bargain, I would have gladly taken away a piano for this guy! Plus, I had a lot less down time compared to having my truck towed away and waiting in line at the mechanic.

Barter works. We traded skill for skill, I mean, if you could call carting away junk a skill. A trade? Profession? Situation? Something anyway. Barter worked out quite well in this case, for the both of us. He also got to do some mechanical work, which you could tell he missed doing.

Chapter 3 – Equipment

The next few sections will discuss the different pieces of equipment that you will find to be useful.

Hand Trucks

You'll need at least one hand truck, but two is ideal. The first kind that you'll want is a general purpose hand truck as shown in the picture below.

Now, I wouldn't go out and just buy one. You'll probably be able to borrow one from a friend for a while, or you might even be able to pick one up cheap either in the newspaper or at a garage sale. You can also visit www.ebay.com or www.craigslist.com to see if there are any deals. If you live in Fairfield County (CT) then grab a copy of the Bargain News when it comes out on Thursday.

Ironically, you'll inevitably do a job where someone will be throwing one of these simpler hand trucks away, guaranteed.

Dave Merton

The next type of hand truck that you'll want is the more advanced kind for moving heavy appliances. 99% of the time the heavy appliance will be a refrigerator.

This style hand truck is ideal, as you can stick a refrigerator on it, and the back wheels will keep it from falling on you. It also has the all-important strap to tie down the refrigerator.

(**Note:** If and when you do die, you can't let it be from a refrigerator falling on you. Your friends will make too much fun of you.)

How To Make Money Doing Junk Removal

This style hand truck may not be the best for what you need. Notice that the D-shaped handlebar section (uppermost) will actually be in the way of a refrigerator.

This one may cost you money. I was in a situation where my room mate had one that he wasn't using. If you do have to buy one, get a used one. They are indestructible, so even if it isn't pretty, as long as it works, who cares what it looks like.

Note: When it comes to refrigerators, there are a few things to remember:

1. They are heavy, get help.
2. See # 1.
3. The rules may vary from one municipality to the other as far as what is involved in the legal removal of a refrigerator. This is because they all contain Freon. In the town where I lived, the cost for dropping off a Freon containing unit (whether it was a refrigerator or even just an air conditioner) was 35 bucks. That was the town's cost to have the Freon evacuated from the unit. Since removing the refrigerators was a royal pain to begin with, and I had to cough up 35 big ones to unload it, I started out charging 100 bucks to get rid of one, but eventually went

35

up to 150. Another junk guy that I knew charged 200. Charging 200 is more of an I-don't-really-want-to-come-and-get-you-fridge price.
4. Last but not least, if you think that you are going to just give away a fridge to a friend, as opposed to paying to get rid of it, or even less likely, that you are going to sell it, do yourself a favor and just get rid of it. Life is too short. I only was able to give away one, and only because it was the antique style type and went into someone's garage. Use refrigerators are usually filthy and disgusting. JUST THROW THEM OUT, legally.

Power Tools

There are a few power tools that you should have available. You don't necessarily have to lug them around with you on every job. In most cases you will be using the power tools when you get back from the job.

The only times that you may need to use a power tool right o site is if you have to either unscrew something to take it apart or to cut something (like long 2x's) so that they fit into your vehicle.

In any event, here are the tools that I found to be helpful.

Chainsaw

Chainsaws are the best when you need to quickly cut long wooden boards, especially when you might be in a situation where there is no power: Far away from house or the power has been disconnected if the house is vacant.

Sawzall

The Sawzall is your best friend for making quick and small cuts when neatness doesn't count. Actually 'Sawzall' is really a product name,

where as 'reciprocating saw' is the actual tool type. The Sawzall is the reciprocating saw made by Milwaukee power tools and is undeniably the best reciprocating saw in the world. Even Chuck Norris won't mess with a Milwaukee Sawzall.

Circular Saw

The circular saw is really the best option in my opinion for cutting up pallets. Note: You really have to be careful cutting pallets with a circular saw. If you are not careful you can cut your fingers off. If you are not sure about this, then don't do it.

Screw Gun

Cordless screw guns (drills) are essential for when you need to dismantle something quickly that is being held together by screws. For all other types of things in need of smashing, may I suggest sledgehammers and or crowbars?

Every guy should have at least two screw guns, and most guys actually have three.

Hand Tools

These are the items that you will least likely need to purchase since you probably own multiple copies of some of these items already.

Tape Measure

Having a smaller tape measure can be handy when you are trying to assess whether or not something will through either a doorway or other opening. You do not need a 25 ft tape measure, but it will work nonetheless if you already have one. A smaller 12 ft tape measure is just fine for most situations.

Crow Bar, Wrecking Bar

There are times when something needs to be persuaded and a crowbar and/or wrecking bar can be handy. They come in several sizes. Most of the wrecking bars that you will use will be used in conjunction with a hammer. Think of them as a dynamic duo. Please see the note below, in this section, about the need for wearing safety glasses.

Below are a few pictures of different types of crowbars and when you might need each particular type of tool.

36 Inch Ripping Bar

The 3 inch ripping bar is my favorite wrecking bar/crowbar of mass destruction. I have one of these, slightly bent and not as pretty as the one shown above, and it has assisted my through dozens and dozens of jobs. I already had one from doing construction, and you may have one or two of these lying around as well. This type of bar is the best all purpose wrecking bar. If you pack only one bar in your junk vehicle, this is the one that you will want.

This type of bar is commonly referred to by all of the following names:

1. Crowbar
2. Ripping Bar
3. Wrecking Bar

Any designation is fine. Nobody really cares what you call it unless you have several different sizes with you. You can even call them buy female names if you want, like "Bessie" or Sadie". As weird as that may sound, no one will make fun of you when you are holding one of these. Feel the respect.

12 Inch Utility Bar

This tool is one of the 'must have' tools for carpenters and remodelers. It is very useful for getting behind flat types of things, like removing trim/molding that will not be going back up. You never know when you might need one of these bars, so you may decide to bring one. It is handy when the 3 inch ripping bar is too long for where you need to rip something apart. (This is kind of like when the room is too small for the pool table, but they put it there anyway, and so on some shots you need to use the little cue stick.)

You can get these very inexpensively at places like Lowes and the Home Chepot.

This type of bar is commonly referred to by all of the following names:

      1. Utility Bar   - Most common, professional name
      2. Wonder Bar   - Model name specific to Stanley Tools
      3. Flat Bar   - You probably get why it's called this

Dave Merton

Cool people just say flat bar. People only say 'utility bar' in front of a customer. 'Wonder Bar' just sounds like something else…

Note: Always where eye protection when you are using a wrecking bar, especially when you are using the wrecking bar in conjunction with a hammer. Some people may think that if they are already wearing eyeglasses then they have enough protection, but is that really wise?

Ask yourself:

"Self, how much did my eyeglasses cost? How much do I enjoy eyeglasses that are scratch and ding free? How much do safety glasses cost at the local Home Chepot?"

Hammer

Generally speaking, you only need hammers for two reasons:

1. Hitting a wrecking bar
2. Making sure that paint cans are on tight

For using wrecking bars

Most people have a smaller 16 oz hammer, or something similar, at the house. You probably will not need to buy one. Hammers of this size are sometimes referred to as 'trim' hammers or 'finish' hammers. They are the most common type of hammer and are the best all purpose type of hammer to have with you.

You can use a smaller finish hammer when beating on a flat bar (utility bar).

I prefer the smaller hammers for paint can closing. The larger hammers can actually rupture the paint cans and make the shape become un-cylindrical. This can cause loss of integrity and loss of paint, which is never good.

For bashing a large 36 in ripping bar I like to use my 30 oz hammer. I use the Estwing 30 oz hammer, simply because I already had one. Some people may refer to these heavier and larger hammers as 'framing' hammers. You can too, but 'framing' insinuates that you are being 'constructive' when in fact when you are using a 30 oz hammer on a junk job you are really being more 'destructive'.

If you only can have one hammer, the smaller one is the way to go, in my opinion.

Safety Glasses

You really need to wear appropriate eye protection when the need arises.

If you already wear eyeglasses you should not think that this is enough proper protection. Eyeglasses are expensive, and can get scratched easily. However, even more valuable than eyeglasses would have to be our eyes and out vision. Please wear safety glasses when applicable. It is a very inexpensive form of insurance.

Some eye protection available today is made to fit right over your eyeglasses. Store bought eye protection is the best. In some cases I've actually used old ski goggles to go over my eyeglasses, but the problem with that is that the goggles are usually tinted, which can dim your view of what you are looking at. I strongly recommend professional eye protection. It is not expensive.

Bolt Cutters

You may only need these once or twice but they are essential when you need them.

I would not suggest investing the cash to buy a pair of bolt cutters if you do not already own a pair. If you know that you are going to need

41

a pair on a job then that might be the time to buy them, or you might even be able to borrow a pair from someone else that may own them.

I am just mentioning them here so that if you already own a pair or have access to a pair that you will know to keep them on your junk vehicle.

Please do not use them to cut locks off of places where you are not authorized to do so, like if and when a storage facility places a security lock on one of your units because the payment was late.

Other

The following section shows some of the more common things that you should have with you. These are items that you most likely already have at your home or office.

Work Gloves

You should always have a few pairs of this that you can slip on. One pair should be a heavy leather pair for touching nasty stuff and another pair should be one of the breathable lighter pairs for general purpose work.

Always use work gloves when using tools with handles, even a push broom. Nothing says 'fun' quite like a monster size splinter.

Safety Vest

These are optional. They are those lightweight yellow vests that civilian workmen wear while directing traffic, like utility pole workers or tree workers.

I had to wear one of these when I dumped stuff at the 'transfer station'. The transfer station is where garbage trucks dump stuff and where dumpsters are emptied out. It is not a landfill per se, but a transfer station. The stuff gets 'transferred'. To where does it get transferred you ask? I haven't the foggiest idea.

This particular transfer station required that you wear a safety vest when unloading your truck. They cost less than $10.00 to buy at the store, but it was $5.00 to 'rent' for a few minutes at the transfer station if you didn't know about the rule. I needed two so that my helper would have one too.

A quick word about safety vests: The first time you wear one and then cross the street, cars will slow down for you just a little more readily than they normally would. This is the magic of the safety vest. When you have it on, people driving in cars just kind of assume that you get to boss them around and tell them what to do. You don't, but they just assume it. It's pretty cool. Please do not take advantage of the safety vest power.

"With great power comes great responsibility" - *Uncle Ben, Spiderman*

Back Brace

Having some type of back support is never a bad idea, especially if you are hefting someone's dearly beloved couch into the back of a truck. There are many options out there, and you should consider what the best option might be for you, if any.

I used to use one of those 'low profile' foam and nylon weightlifting belts. It worked fine for me. I used that type because I already owned it. This way I was protecting my back w/o having to spend additional money.

Also, the foam/nylon belts are more practical than the leather ones because they are washable. That being said, I don't think that I ever actually washed mine.

Dave Merton

Rope

The rope is not for Colonel Mustard in the Observatory, or for annoying customers or annoying helpers. It is really handy for tying off sleeper sofas so that when you need to move them that they don't decide to open up on you when you tilt them. You really need to tie off the couches, or you will be unhappy, especially if the sleeper sofa decides to unfold on you when you are carrying it down a set of stairs. This can ruin an afternoon.

Trash Bags

You may need contractor bags on big jobs and also for throwing away large bags of trash.

Note: Paying for a weekly trash service is one of the most cost effective ways of regularly getting rid of smaller amounts of junk. Back in my heyday I was having trash service 2 times a week. It was the bomb. I also would tip the trash guys regularly in appreciation for their hard work. Three or four singles, folded up a little looks like a huge wad of cash.

Chapter 4 – Vehicles

The next few sections will cover the different types of vehicles that are good to have when engaging in junk removal.

Vans

I used a van when I first got started. (It had belonged to a contractor, so you know that it wasn't pampered. I found it in the Bargain News for 900 bucks. It was already pretty much retired, but I gave that old dog a whole new purpose in life.)

Commandment # 4
Think big, pay small!

A van is fine and will serve you well. A van is an excellent choice for a first vehicle for your fleet. My van was similar to the one displayed below, except that mine had less windows, and was not an extended van. An extended van would have been supremely better. Every extra inch is like a mile when it comes to playing Tetris with your available space. My rig did have the same beautiful blending of cream and rust though. The van shown below is missing a few all-important dents, but nothing's perfect I suppose.

Commandment # 5
Think like you're playing Tetris; Stack Nice!

There are pros and cons of course; however the pros definitely outweigh the cons as you will see:

Dave Merton

Pros

1. A decent used van is usually easily obtained for less than a 1000 bucks.
2. A van is enclosed, so you don't have to worry about debris flying out the back when you are screaming down the freeway. You also don't have to worry about people stealing your valuables. (wait for laughter, wait for it) Actually, a portion of the booty will be valuable, so this is a solid point.

Cons

1. A van is limited in size both volumetrically as well as geometrically. Stick a couch and a fridge inside one ad then just try to start packing other items. They might all fit, if you used maybe a wood chipper, but not as they are. (Don't forget, depending on the logistics of the job, you could always make multiple trips.)

Commandment # 6

When making multiple trips, plan with the destination in mind before planning with the packing of the vehicle in mind.

Box Trucks

A box truck is really a necessity if you are going to be doing any serious junk removal. Just make sure to hide the truck from view whenever your friends are moving.

Box trucks can have several different names:

1. Box truck

2. Straight truck
3. High cube van
4. Cutaway Van
5. Homeless Shelter

Okay, that least one is unofficial.

They are legally driven with a normal driver's license. The do not have the air braking system that tractor trailers have, they are really just an over sized square vans. The picture below is a typical box truck from U-Haul:

Most box trucks do not come with the little overhang section over the cab, they just have a big 'cube' section; hence the term 'Cutaway'.

When it comes to doing a large job in one single trip, the box truck is your best weapon of mass junk removal. You just need to be mindful of road signs that you never used to see before, like the ones that see that an overpass is 9 feet 6 inches, when your box truck is 10 feet. If you get stuck under a bridge, there is like no forgiveness from the local law enforcement. Rumor has it that it is the largest ticket that you will ever get.

I might have hit a building with a box truck once, but that was for a different job, in a different box truck, and it was actually the main structural support in parking garage, which was holding up an entire shopping mall in West Hartford. So, let me just state with 100% certainty that you can't pass a taller vehicle under a shorter passageway any time of day, any day of the year. I was only off by like 2 inches. Math doesn't care. Two inches may as well be two feet.

Read the signs.

Dave Merton

Rentals

From time to time you may need to rent, like if your van/box truck becomes unusable due to either being full, or being sick. It happens.

BTW, before we get started on this section, I would like to point out that renting a UHaul truck can be a nice alternative to buying a truck when you are first starting out. If you get a few nice jobs in the $400 - $500 range, and are smart about how you unload the junk, then you might be able to locate a usable vehicle to purchase with those funds. You may have to look around. Don't ever buy a vehicle just because you need one for a job, or because it's convenient; buy one because the price is great. Both my vehicles, a van and a box truck, were under a thousand. I found them both in the print edition of the Bargain News.

Now, when you do rent, you will need a folder of some kind, preferably a pouch with a zipper, but that's up to you. You need this because you need to save the receipts for the rental as well as the gas that you put into it. You need to save receipts too if you get stuck adding oil or antifreeze. All those costs are deductable; however the mileage isn't, because it's not your truck. Be smart and write 'Rental' on the top of all of the receipts as soon as you get it. Then pouch it. When you're done renting the truck, staple all of the receipts right onto the rental receipt and then tuck that puppy in with all your other tax info for the year.

My experience has been that U-Haul has the best rates. They also have some of the most hideous looking trucks. That's fine, it adds to the whole experience.
Just a quick note on renting: Don't just show up when you need a truck, they could all be rented out and heading to Florida. Oh, if you happen to be in Florida, then they are all probably heading to Texas. What's up with Texas? Is it the new Arizona or something?

Different rental places have different clientele types, some have no trucks during the week and some have no trucks on the weekend. This may surprise you. It surprised me.

The best thing to do is go in at least two days in advance, assuming that you know two days in advance. Explain too that you will possibly be renting more than once, and that it's local. They love when it's a cross country rental, because they make a killing, but they'll like local if you tell them that you might be back earlier in the day. Then they can rent it out again. I've found that you really need to communicate with these guys. Even if they say that they have no trucks for a certain day, a little bit of brainstorming (some might call it badgering) can go a long way.

When selecting the right truck, size matters. Don't just think volume, think convenience. A twelve ft length of rolled up carpet just doesn't place nice when you are trying to Tetris all those square pieces of furniture together. Spending another few bucks is much more advisable than having to make two long, gas guzzling trips to the junk site, just because the truck was too small.

BTW, the rates vary depending on where you rent, but from what I just read on line each of these trucks below has a $.89 fee per mile, and a base rental fee. The ten ft truck is only $19.95 where as the 14 ft truck is $29.95. When it comes to junk, trust me on this, normal arithmetic does not apply. You can pack TWICE as much in the 14 ft truck. For another ten bucks, that's the deal of the century.

10 ft   14 ft

To see more details, go here:
http://www.uhaul.com/reservations/RatesTrucks.aspx

I've personally rented almost every size, partly depending on the specific junk job, but also because sometimes it's a question of availability.

Make sure before you rent it that the loading ramp actually deploys. Rental vehicles are not known for receiving the same care that you would give to fully restored '73 Corvette, so they do get pounded on from time to time. Check the ramp.

Also, for the extra few bucks, get a hand truck if you do not already have one. For local rentals a small hand truck is only seven bucks and an appliance dolly is only ten.

One quick note for safety. ONLY USE AN APPLIANCE DOLLY WHEN MOVING APPLIANCES. YOU MUST ADHERE TO THIS. GET ALL THE ADDITIONAL HELP THAT YOU NEED FROM OTHER PEOPLE.

How To Make Money Doing Junk Removal

Commandment #7

ALWAYS USE AN APPLIANCE DOLLY WHEN MOVING AN APPLIANCE!

Commandment #8

ALWAYS GET ALL THE ADDITIONAL HELP THAT YOU NEED FROM OTHER PEOPLE WHEN YOU ARE MOVING HEAVY APPLIANCES!

Vehicle Write Offs

This is just a quick section on how I calculated write offs for my vehicles. I just want to state again that I am not an accountant or an attorney and I am in no way offering professional advice on this topic. I am merely telling you what made sense to me when I used a pencil, piece of paper and a calculator. (Actually, it was Microsoft Excel.) So please, speak to your accountant.

Also, this information has to do with vehicles that either you or your business owns. This information is not applicable to rental vehicles, like U-Haul or Penske. In those cases, you need to keep all of the receipts, both for rental and then for gassing it up before returning it.

When you first put a vehicle "into service" for a business, you have to decide how you will be calculating write offs for the vehicle. We will assume that it is strictly a work vehicle. There are really two choices, you can track all expenses (gas, insurance, etc) or you can track mileage. Every situation is different. If you just paid cash for a brand new $40,000.00 box truck (which you shouldn't...) versus someone like me who found a fully functioning (and very beat on) Chevy Vandura 1989 Box Truck then the strategy would be different.

Dave Merton

With the new vehicle you would not want to do mileage, you would want to do cost either all at once or depreciation. Again, this is where having a sharp accountant comes in handy.

If you do mileage, then you cannot deduct the overall cost. With a major vehicle purchase, mileage will kill you. The costs to purchase the vehicle will be much greater than the write off value of mileage, unless you drive over a million miles in one year. BW, if you *are* driving over a million miles in one year, then you probably are not approaching this business in the correct way.

With a $700.00 piece-of-junk truck like mine, mileage is a dream come true. It is a true gift from the IRS.

Here's why: During 2012 the mileage allowance was, I believe, 0.55½ per mile. That means that whether you have a brand new 40K box truck, or a POJ $700 special like mine, mileage is mileage. I would get the same write off *per mile* as new truck guy. Doesn't that almost seem unfair? The new truck makes people smile as it flies down the road. My truck made people wary and nauseous. Same deduction though. For me it was like getting free money at tax time.

If you find a vehicle cheap enough, and use it enough, and if it never breaks down, you could actually end up writing off more than the vehicle ever cost you, especially in subsequent years. I'm talking about gas, insurance and registration fees too.

I came pretty close to this one year. Think about it: If gas is $4.00 a gallon and if your big box truck averages a whopping 12 mpg, loaded, then it costs you $4.00 to go 12 miles, however you get to write off $6.66 (0.55½ * 12) for that 12 miles. (Sorry about the creepiness of $6.66, it just worked out that way…) That means that you would be writing off more than what it cost you to gas up your vehicle. If you have smaller vehicles, like a van or a pickup truck, the math even gets better.

My goal was to keep my vehicle costs down. Also, for junk removal, you really don't have to have a spiffy looking vehicle. It's almost like

the one time when it's cool to have a 'rickety' looking rig. People will think that perhaps you will not overcharge them when they see your less-than-pristine unit.

BTW, if you think that you won't be able to find a vehicle like my box truck or the Ford van that I found for only $900.00, guess again. There are deals out there. They are everywhere. You may have to look a little. I looked at only 1 van when I bought the Ford, and it was from Litchfield, CT, about a half hour from my home. The box truck was from Hamden, about an hour from my home. This also was the first box truck that I looked at. Both were ads from the Bargain News, a CT paper.

Be creative. I know of a friend who saw a pickup just sitting* in an industrial park. I talked to someone that I knew, who knew the owner, and the next thing I knew, my friend this truck for parts. The price? The guy offered to just give it away! My friend still gave him a couple hundred. This was a win/win for both parties. People junk vehicles every day, so the potential is out there. Find these trucks before they get junked. You'll be so glad you did.

* You need to be observant. People's needs change all the time.

Chapter 5 – Advertising

This section deals with advertising, but it also deals with a closely related item: The initial communication with the customer. It is vital to understand how this needs to work. We will touch on both items in this section.

There are a few tricks to advertising for junk removal. The goal is this: You want to get the greatest amount of phone calls for the least amount of dollars.

> **Commandment # 9**
>
> **You need to get the greatest amount of calls for the least amount of dollars.**

When people do call, then what should you do? Find out what they have, where they live, and then set up an appointment to take a look. DO NOT GIVE OUT PRICES OVER THE PHONE!
Note: Never sell over the phone! Sell the appointment, not the job!

> **Commandment # 10**
>
> **DO NOT GIVE OUT PRICES OVER THE PHONE!**

This is critical to understand, otherwise you could get creamed on an over-the-phone estimate. When they say: "Could you just at least give me a ball park?" you need to say these simple words without any deviation: "I'm sorry, but I would really need to see it personally." Then immediately offer to come over right away, later in the day, or the following day.

People usually don't have a clear concept as to how this chain of events works. That is why they will usually innocently ask you to give them an idea of cost over the phone, before you can see what's involved. That's crazy, you are not omniscient.

It's not just what is being removed, but how difficult it is to get it to your truck. You might have to carry stuff down stairs, or across a ridiculously huge yard, etc.

When it comes to a removal job, house to truck logistics is just as important as the amount of junk that is involved.

Marketing note: The goal of advertising is to create traffic, not sales. (Huh?) That may sound strange, but the purpose of advertising is to bring a potential customer and a seller together. That's it! Once they are together, the advertising has done its job, the rest is up to you. If you get ten calls, and only sell two jobs, then it's not the advertising's fault, it's yours. That just means that you need to learn how to sell.

Your odds of closing the deal are astronomically better if you are on site. You will usually have the option of removing the junk right away or setting up another mutually convenient time. Either way, you win.

Paper Advertising

In the next few sections I both discuss and compare a few different paper publications.

The Housatonic Weekender

I loved advertising in the local weekend paper that was delivered free of charge to the local town. It went out on Friday, which meant that folks would be looking it over on Saturday morning while drinking their coffee. Saturday mornings I would usually average about three to four calls just from this paper which was phenomenal!

For only 74 bucks, they would run a business card ad 4 times, meaning 4 weeks. The actual ad was slightly larger than a real business card, which was nice too.

Below is the ad that I ran. Feel free to use it. I blocked out my cel.

I'm going to go over several reasons why this ad worked so well. There are three sets of reasons. The first set of reasons is specific to the paper that I was running it in, the second set of reasons has to do with the ad itself, while the third set is not specific to either of the other two sets.

The actual paper itself

1. The paper was laid out well and had a great readership
2. The ads were big and the price was small
3. It was delivered on Friday, which meant that Saturday morning, folks would read it.

The ad itself

1. It says in huge letter 'JUNK REMOVAL', which grabs attention.
2. It is black on white, with heavy contrasts (so it stands out on the page).

3. It gives an idea of what can be taken, area served
4. It is humorous, you have to do this!
5. It has an offer*. You need to have an offer. Now it's a coupon, and not just an ad. People will save the ad for years if they know that they will be moving.

* BTW: I picked $20 as an offer for two reasons:

1. A low dollar figure makes people think that it's reasonable. Using a percent for a discount just makes people think that you are marking it up the day before, like the furniture guys or the jewelry stores.
2. Some other dude was offering $15 off.

The ad in general

1. It says "Junk Removal". This was already stated; however it is being restated here for a different reason. Most people don't know that this type of business even exists.

During my stint with this paper, I made out really well. The overall cost for a job was a little over $6 bucks, which is a tremendous return on investment! My average job was probably about 150 to 180 bucks in profit, not counting reselling stuff. BTW, Jobs can range in cost from $50, my minimum, to $3000 or more.

Oh, on a sad note, the cost per job was great, but this publication was bought out by a much larger one and then has since vanished. Poof! It may be entirely possible that they were not charging enough for their ads. The pricing model may not have been sustainable, especially since they were also printing some news as well.

The Yankee Pennysaver

I also had very good success with a journal called the Yankee Pennysaver, which is based in Brookfield, CT.

The Yankee Pennysaver was great as well. My job acquisition cost was at about $20 per job. That is still great, believe me. I would do that all day long.

Out of the two paper publications that were mentioned, only the Yankee Pennysaver has survived the test of time. The Housatonic Weekender was bought out and then went 'away'. Perhaps they were not profitable and their model was not sustainable. (But it was fun while it lasted!)

The Yankee Pennysaver continues to succeed despite a less than stellar economy. This is proof that their publication works and that their advertisers are happy to continue investing advertising dollars with them. This is a testament to the vision and marketing wisdom of the journal's two publishers.

Besides the two publications that were mentioned, I did try ads in other paper publication, but I will not name them, because the results were not that great.

BTW, get into the habit of asking your customers how they heard about you.

Yellow Pages

I never spent a dime on the yellow pages. I decided not to do it for 3 reasons:

1. The ads are not cheap
2. People in general aren't aware of the junk removal business, so they don't know to look for it. This is all the reason that you need.
3. In the yellow pages, under 'Junk', is just a list of folks who toe away cars.

Dave Merton

I am not knocking the yellow pages. I think they are great, and have been for several years. It's just that you need to be engaged in a business that people are aware of, like Painting or Legal Advice.

Business Cards

Get a ton of these, at least a 1000. Leave them everywhere. I'm going to mention a few specific places below in two other sections. Don't go crazy, just get black and white, it's cheaper. Use the ad I supplied above, it really works. Include an offer. Don't go crazy, $20 off is fine.

Realtors

Stop by every realty office and let them know what you do. Leave your cards with individual realtors if they are around.

The jobs may take a little time to trickle in, but when they do, you really need to take care of these realtors, because they will bring you the biggest jobs. This is because families will be moving, and need to unload lots and lots of junk. ☺

Lastly, this type of advertising is essentially free, minus the pennies in cost for the business cards left with them.

Homes for Sale

I would knock on doors of houses with 'For Sale' signs, when I had the time. If they weren't home, I'd leave my card.

This had okay results, but again, like the realtor strategy, the cost is pennies.

Long Term Benefits of Advertising

This is something that you will grow to love. You'll eventually hear from people that they kept your ad for a year or more because they knew that they'd need to call you when they had to move. Most folks in that position are afraid that your ad might not be there in a year or two. In most folks minds, junk removal is a fly-by-night gig. It's funny when you get calls that start out with: "Do you still do this?"

Truck Lettering

Never advertise on your vehicle! Lettering looks like it costs too much (you are not an electrician). Don't give other people (entrepreneurs) any ideas. For the cost of lettering on a vehicle, you could invest in several ads. Think about that.

Chapter 6 – Pickups

This chapter is closely related to the next chapter, which discusses how to get rid of junk. It would almost have been better to switch the order of this chapter and the next chapter, except for the fact that you really need to get junk before you can get rid of junk.

There are three overall questions that you will need to answer when organizing and planning your junk jobs for the day or week:

1. Will I need help on a particular job?
2. Which vehicle(s) will I need? – If you have a choice.
3. In what order should I load stuff onto the vehicle?
4. Does it matter what order I do the jobs in?

Each of these questions will be addressed below in its own section.

Will I Need Help on a Particular Job?

This is the easiest of these questions to answer. It is basically a matter of whether or not you need to move a heavy item, like a couch or a refrigerator.

There are other times where you may want to bring a helper as well. These are the times when perhaps there is a lot of manual labor, like several trips from the house to the truck, like when you are helping someone move.

There may be other issues as well, such as less daylight during certain parts of the year, or you just need to be in different places at different times and can't get the work done by yourself.

Helpers will be easier to comer by if you give them a little notice and a good chunk of change per hour.

Dave Merton

Which Vehicle(s) Will I Need?

In my case I had a ford van and a box truck. The van was great for smaller jobs, and it could actually fit a couch and or a mattress, but those items would fill it up quickly. Any jobs where there were lots of item and some of them were large items, like appliances, I would take the box truck.

You might wonder why I wouldn't always simply take the box truck, since it is bigger. The van was ideal for smaller jobs as well as it used much less gas. Also, if I am collecting different types of junk from different jobs and these different types of junk have different 'destinies' then it makes sense to use the different vehicles.

In What Order Should I Load Stuff onto the Vehicle(s)?

This part is basically all common sense. Also, no one can definitively tell you in advance how to best do every packing job. You will need to determine that when you are on site. I can however tell you some of the important principles that will help guide you.

There are two overall concepts: Item packing and destination packing. Each of these items will be discussed below.

Item packing

Item packing assumes that everything that you will be packing will be going to the same place when the truck is unloaded. This is very similar in approach to when you are loading a moving van, with the exception that if stuff breaks, nobody cares.

Load all of the big, heavy or bulky items first, like big appliances, furniture, couches or even rolled up carpet. Depending on how full you will be loading the vehicle you can either put mattresses in first,

against a side wall (upright) or you can try and lay them on top at the end. If you lay them on top, at the end, just make sure that they don't come crashing down on you when you open the truck later on. Also, if you are not careful the mattresses can cause issues trying to open the truck back up if they are packed to high and then shift around.

Destination Packing

Destination packing takes into account the different possible drop off locations that you may have in mind for the different junk types that you are loading.

For example, let's say that you have a truckload of stuff that will primarily be going to either a dumpster, dump or a transfer station. The only exceptions are a few paint cans with liquid paint still in them and a large air conditioner. The air conditioner has Freon and the paint cans have paint so they are not allowed to be dumped. You need to think about what will be gotten rid of first and then pack the truck in reverse order.

If your next stop is going to be the dump, then stick the air conditioner and the paint cans way in the back, so that they will be out of the way and then you can deal with them afterwards. If you packed them last then you would be tripping over them and would have to move them off the truck and then back on which is extra work. This means that you would be tripping over them in the meantime. Plus, it could appear as though you were trying to dump toxic items at the dump. That could be very bad.

On the other hand, if you were going to drop the air conditioner off a t a local recycling center first, and then go to the dump, then you would instead want to pack the air conditioner unit last so that you could easily grab it right off the truck.

Destination packing trumps item packing in the order of importance.

Dave Merton

Does It Matter What Order I Do Jobs In?

Yes. If you have two jobs to do where one of them is just a couch and the other is a bunch of small and/or odd sized items, then get the couch first, since it will be much easier to position against a nice clean wall lf the truck. Think of Tetris and stack nice.

Chapter 7 – Disposal - Getting Rid Of Stuff

This is one of the most important phases of the junk removal business. It is *the phase* that you need to spend the most time thinking about, as this portion of the business tends to be more 'fluid', meaning that situations, conditions and scenarios can change every day. One day you may load the truck one way, whereas the next day you may approach it differently, because other circumstances have changed.

This chapter cannot possibly diagram how you will choose to execute your plan of operations on a day by day basis. Instead, it will merely give you the basics and some food for thought regarding the different vectors of junk unloading.

This aspect of the business will always be the most satisfying for you and will make you smile the most when you do it right. This is because you will need to be smart, alert and creative all at the same time. It is the true hallmark of the entrepreneur.

The way that we will approach this chapter is twofold. First we will discuss the different ways to unload junk, other than the money making ways that were previously discussed in **Chapter 2 - 10 Ways to Make Money**. Next we will discuss the three different vectors of getting rid of junk: The quick, the cheap and the easy. (Sounds like a Clint Eastwood movie title a little. BTW, my father resembled Clint Eastwood when he was younger, but, um, I did not.)

So, just to classify this, we will be discussing these four over all ideas:

1. Personal Circumstances
2. How and/or where to unload (get rid of) junk
3. Unloading specific items
4. Getting rid of junk *quickly*, *cheaply* and *easily*

Let's now look at each of these ideas in more detail.

First we will discuss how personal circumstances can have a bearing on your junk removal business.

Then we will cover some of the many places/ways to unload junk.

Finally we will discuss more details for some specific types of junk.

Personal Circumstances

We will now discuss how personal circumstances can have a bearing on your junk removal business. We will be covering how differences in the following personal circumstances may impact your ability to do certain things in regard to junk removal. This is just a rough guide, please do not attempt to radically change your circumstances (like buy a new home or get rid of an old spouse) just to better fit these circumstances. Take these following thoughts in stride.

1. Family dynamics
2. Type of home
3. Location
4. Parking

Family Dynamics & Type of Home

It should not seem strange that we are addressing these two items simultaneously. If it does, no worries, that just means that you are most likely a clueless single male. (Are there other types?) That's fine, that's the perfect demographic for doing junk removal and the following info will not really apply to you. Go get a beer and skip ahead.

I mention the family dynamics, because if married guys tried to pull the same things as single guys, then the marriage might be in jeopardy. Don't get divorced over junk removal. No one will take your side. Ever. Just sayin'.

How To Make Money Doing Junk Removal

Okay, so if you live in a mobile home or in an apartment on the 88th floor of a skyscraper you may not have as much available 'storage space' as say someone who lives in a rural area with a 2 car garage and/or a large empty barn. Life isn't fair.

If you rent a room (like I did) from a friend as opposed to owning a home, you will be more limited as well. This is especially true if the friend is uptight. (I say that completely randomly.)

If you like to 'temporarily' shove stuff in the garage until you can deal with it, then a spouse may have an issue with it. Especially since some people have different definitions of words like 'temporary'.

If you *do* have a situation where you have some 'temporary' storage space available to you that will not rock the boat or step on anyone's toes or make neighbors want to snipe you then you will be able to really maximize some of my tricks for getting rid of junk more cheaply.

Location

Location, in this regard, has to do more with the kind of street that you live *on* as opposed to the type of building that you live *in*. If you live on a busier street of a rural town, where you can put free items outside without breaking any laws, then that is infinitely better than if you live at the end of a dead end street in the middle of nowhere. If that's the case then you will need to make friends with someone who has a location that gets a lot of traffic.

It will really be helpful if the space that you use for letting go of 'free' stuff is close to your home. Ideally it should be your home if you live in a busy area. This way you can keep an eye on it all.

Alternatively the 'free' space should be near where you park your vehicle, since you may have to reload whatever items were not taken away.

73

Dave Merton

Parking

Parking is a concern if you have a truck or two. If you have a big box truck, some neighbors will freak out if you park it in a rural neighborhood. I had a place in town, half a mile away where I was able to park for free for a while. Eventually I had to move it. The truck was becoming, how should I say this, quite famous in and around my town.

Parking is something that you don't want to end up paying for, because it costs you money even when you are not working.

Lastly, don't think that you can indefinitely park a huge box truck on a steep hill if that's your only place. Fully loaded the truck is heavier and eventually the parking brake may fail. Nothing could be worse than a runaway box truck full of junk. That will not be a soothing thought if you already suffer from insomnia. Try to find a place that is flat, free and secure. They exist in most places.

Lastly, it really helps when this parking spot is close to your home and/or close to your most popular dumping locations.

Where to Unload Stuff

Each person's junk removal business will vary depending on where they are located simply because dumping options vary from one locale to the next. You need to become extremely familiar with what is available in your territory. The following is a list of the different options that I have used in the past in Connecticut. This is not a complete list, but the list of the most popular methods.

1. Recycling Center
2. Transfer Station / Dump
3. Trash Service
4. Free Sign

Following will be a brief section on less frequently used options:

1. Dumpster
2. Brush

Each of these will be discussed in more detail below. Note: At times I would temporarily put items into storage if I was not yet ready to dump them. This can work out well for you, however storage does cost money (if you are renting the space) and should only be used when absolutely necessary.

So, first we will go over the more frequently used venues.

Recycling Center

Most towns and smaller cities will have some kind of Recycling Center.

Usually you need to live in the town or own property in the town to dump in the town's recycling center.

Every town is different when it comes to pricing. In my town we had to purchase a windshield sticker once per year (per vehicle) to drive through the recycling center. It was something like $10.00 - $15.00. Since I had a car and two trucks, I had to shell this out 3 times.

What was nice about this recycling center is that they took just about everything. Some things cost money, other things did not. You could freely dump all household recyclables like plastic and glass containers, cardboard & newspapers. Some items that were still in good condition, like end tables, toys and books could be placed on a 'free' table. This meant that it was free to leave the items as well as free to take them. Whether or not something was deemed 'worthy' of being left for free on the free table was up to the discretion of whoever was running the front gate at the time. The gate guys were usually pretty reasonable as long as I wasn't trying to take advantage of the free table. (This is the part of the movie where I clear my throat and look off to the side…)

Dave Merton

We were also allowed to leave metal for free, like bed frames and metal shelves, grills that had the charcoal dumped out and the propane tanks removed. Dishwashers were only $5.00 and couches were $10.00 or more depending on if they were sleeper sofas.

Air conditioners and refrigerators were $35.00 a piece, and this was exactly what the town had to pay a company to come by and evacuate the Freon, so it was really a gift that the town did not add a surcharge.

Contractor bags were $5.00 to dump and I never loaded one that wasn't completely full. I can almost load a used car into a contractor bag, those things are huge.

I used the recycling center for a lot of my dumping. I made the most trips there, as it was less than a mile from my house and my trucks.

The only place where I either dumped more or spent more was the transfer station, which will be covered in the next section. I made fewer trips to the transfer station, but dumped lots more per trip.

There was one type of dumping at the recycling center that was a little pricey. It was called 'bulky waste'. Bulky waste was basically anything that couldn't fall into any one of the other areas. It was usually stuff like huge chunks of carpet or construction debris, like sheetrock and plywood scraps. This was the one time where the Recycling Center made money. You basically had to load your stuff into the bucket of a backhoe. I think it was a three yard bucket, so it was huge, like a snow plow, not like the small bucket that you initially may think of. Anyway, if you filled the bucket, it was $80.00. Trust me, that's expensive. If you only have a pickup truck then it's the only option you have to dump your stuff. I had to use this a few times for convenience sake, because I may not have had enough junk to justify a trip to the transfer station. To avoid the costliness of the bulky waste fees I got smart and learned how to dump this type of stuff through the normal weekly trash. You will see exactly what I am talking about when you read the section below called *Trash Service*.

Transfer Station / Dump

This was the biggest and best way to dump monster trash. It was the big league way.

Just a little clarification: A transfer station is very similar to a dump or a land fill. For all intents and purposes to you they are the same. It may cost you a hair more, and you don't get to see a new mountain growing on the horizon due to your efforts, but otherwise it's the same deal. You drive over a scale to get the full weight. Then you dump out your stuff get back in line and then get weighed again empty. Finally you pay and you leave. They even have seagulls like at the dump. The only difference is that at a transfer station the junk gets to go on one more mission before it dies. It gets shipped to another location.

I would load my box truck to the gills whenever I went to the transfer station to maximize the value. This is because you had to pay a flat fee plus a fee based on the weight of what you dumped. I think the flat fee was $150.00. That was just to show up and drive over the scale. After dumping you would get reweighed and then also pay for the weight at so much per every 100 pounds.

I could drive out of there with an empty truck after having paid a total of say $250-$260. That beats having to get a dumpster for $500. BTW, this is the same place where the dumpster guys drop their stuff, so it would have to be cheaper for me.

It would never make sense to load a van and then go there; it would just cost too much money. You would need to have a fully loaded box truck.

There are a few things that you need to know about this type of dumping. First, you need to have one of those Gatorade yellow safety vests. If you don't splurge and pay the $9.00 at the store then they will happily rent you one for $5.00 for 15 minutes.

Also, you really need to bring a helper. This is for two reasons. The first is timing. It takes a little while to unload a box truck by yourself

and there will be several trucks waiting in line behind you. A helper will speed this up. Also, you will usually be parked on a large metal platform when you are unloading if you are at a transfer station, as opposed to 'soil' at a dump or landfill. This means that you have to quickly sweep off the areas so that you don't drive over huge framing spikes or nails. I know one another junk guy who claims to have gotten 3 flats on the same trip to the transfer station because of nails. Ow. Keep a push broom on the truck where you can immediately grab it.

Trash Service

This turned out to be one of my best financial decisions in the junk removal business. This trash company charged me only $33.00 a month to pick up trash every week. That means 4 times a month with the occasional 5th time a month depending on how the calendar was looking.

This might not sound like a huge deal, but let me tell you what they took. I was allowed to fill 4 large trash barrels and then 2 contractor bags on top of it. That sounded too good to be true, but it wasn't. Do you have any idea how much crap you can stuff into 4 large trash barrels plus 2 contractor bags? A lot! Nowadays, on the street that I used to live on everyone has to use these plastic wheelie bins. I never could have packed as much stuff into a wheelie bin as 4 large trash barrels and 2 contractor bags. It would've taken like 3 wheelie bins at least.

To dump a full contractor bag down at the recycling center it was $5.00. With the trash guys it was running me on average $7.61 per week for the 4 barrels and 2 bags. What a deal! It was so good that after a while I expanded to twice a week. The garbage company started to get suspicious, so if you do this, go with two different companies on two different days.

I don't think that they pick up that much stuff anymore for $33.00 and I bet that I am part of the reason why they don't!

One quick note: If I had some extra heavy stuff in the barrels I would wait out front and offer to help the guys dump it. Also, if I had even more stuff, or something big and questionable I would tip the guys. I believe in tipping, just like Vincent Antonelli in *My Blue Heaven*.

When you tip the trash guys get maybe three to four singles and kinda fold them up. Keep it under $5.00 so that it is easier on the pocket and then you can do it more often. The reasons I liked using singles (even if it was $5.00 or more) were that it looks like more money and also they could split it up if they wanted. There was always an older guy as the driver and then 1 to 2 younger guys riding on the back to look cool and help the environment by breathing in the diesel exhaust fumes.

When you tip them in the spring you will be the only person doing it. They will love you. It shows respect. Don't put the cash in an envelope. That's a sign that you watch too much *Sopranos*.

Free Sign

Anything that is in good enough condition where you can stick it out on the lawn with a free sign and have people take it away for you will basically equate to money in your pocket. Nothing will ever make you feel better than to see free stuff on your lawn disappear.

Don't discount this avenue of removal. Everyone who takes from your free pile today may pay you to pick the stuff up in a year or two. ☺

Now we will briefly discuss some of the less frequently used venues.

Dumpster

I used dumpster maybe twice in my career. This is only because I almost never have enough stuff to actually fill one at the same time and also because they are expensive. I was better off just going to the transfer station myself.

Brush

We had a place in our town that made mulch and you could drop of brush for a very nominal fee. I also had a friend who let me dump brush behind his back yard because he actually was trying to fill in a small valley area. I was more than happy to help.

Don't be afraid to ask around with people that you know. There are always folks looking to mulch and compost.

Specific Items

Following is a short list of how you can get rid of certain specific items.

Propane Tanks

I would recommend taking these to an actual gas company. They used to charge me $5.00 per tank to take them. This was a bargain, as I hate holding on to things that can potentially go boom. Also, I would just add the $5.00 right to my overall price.

Barbecues / Grills

Once you get rid of the propane tank the rest of the grill is usually metal. The tops are often aluminum and can be scrapped.

Be careful when moving and/or touching barbecue grills that have been dormant for any length of time. This is because bees and wasps seem to really like then and tend to build hives and nests in them.

Mattresses

If you want to save a few bucks you can actually take a box spring apart. The springs are completely recyclable/scrappable because they are metal. The wood can usually be burned as it is not finished. The rest of the mattress at that point can be placed into garbage bags.

I've done this before, but it is a little extra work. It's certainly an option if you are running very low on cash.

I've also heard rumors of people using parts of the box springs like rebar in small concrete pours. I would never recommend this, since a building inspector would probably go ballistic, but it does demonstrate that with a little forethought many things can be repurposed.

Couches

Like mattresses, couches can actually be taken apart. Sleepers have metal and it can all be recycled. The rest is usually wood and material. It is usually a lot of work and it may just be smarter to pay the recycling center the $10.00 to $20.00 to take the couch as is; however breaking it down is an option.

Paint Cans

Actually, paint cans are metal and may be recycled, it's the liquid paint that is the problem. There is no good way to get rid of it. I usually ended up giving paint away to people that did crafts. I occasionally kept some. The only alternative is to use it up, or try and dry it out. I do not know of any way to really do this other than killing a Saturday by rolling paint onto old sheets of plywood. That's kind of like hitting rock bottom.

Dave Merton

My approach to this was to tell customers that it was $10.00 per can of liquid paint, no matter how much was in each can. This minimized how many cans I had to take and re-gift to others.

One last thing: Even if paint 'looks' dry, you need to stick a nail or a screw driver into the can to see if the paint near the bottom is also dry. The top can have a dry looking skin, like pudding but the inside can still be liquid. If you try dumping liquid paint anywhere, trash guys, people working in the recycling centers and even folks at the dump will not be happy. You really need to make sure that it is dry.

Getting Rid of Junk <u>Quickly</u>, <u>Cheaply</u> and <u>Easily</u>

This is one of the most important aspects of junk removal, because it translates into both personal profits and personal happiness. You will need to spend the some time thinking about this portion of the business since it tends to be more 'fluid'. This means that situations, conditions and scenarios can change every day. One day you may load the truck one way, whereas the next day you may approach it differently, because other circumstances have changed.

This section cannot possibly diagram how you will choose to execute your plan of operations on a day by day basis. Instead, it will merely give you the basics and some food for thought regarding the different vectors of junk unloading.

This aspect of the business will always be the most satisfying for you and will make you smile the most when you do it right. This is because you will need to be smart, alert and creative all at the same time. It is the true hallmark of the entrepreneur.

The next portion of this chapter will be broken down into specific sections:

1. Getting rid of junk *quickly*...
2. Getting rid of junk *cheaply*...
3. Getting rid of junk *easily*...

There can be a bit of overlap in regard to these different sections, such as with doing jobs quickly and easily. However, there can also be times where one dynamic can cancel out another. In these cases, you must make the call.

Getting Rid of Junk *Quickly*

Junk removal, like any other business, presents you with a plethora of operational decisions. On every job you may need to decide upon the best way to get rid of stuff. Also, as you will learn, this aspect of the business can become quite fluid. You always need to be on the lookout for new opportunities.

That being said, I have found that there certainly are times when getting a job (or even a specific task of an overall job) finished quicker is better, even if it ends up costing you a few dollars in the long run.

What you will learn through trial and error is that it is often wise to have a helper when you need one or even when it just makes the job go more smoothly. In addition, the cheapest place to dump may not always be the best if it takes you more time. We will go into more detail about these two areas:

1. Do you need help?
2. Pennywise and *time* foolish?

Let's take a look at these two areas.

Do You Need Help?

I love when people ask me this when I am at the store or a fast food place. They might word it as, "Are you being helped?" I love it because I get to come back with, "Well, I'm seeing a therapist…"

Well, this manual is *not* about therapy; however this section *is* about getting help when you need it. Granted, there will be times when you will need to have help, like when you have to carry a sofa down a few flights of stairs or when you have to pull a refrigerator out of a basement. What you really need to take to heart though, is that there are other times when you should also have a helper. Sometimes it is just a matter of convenience and/or saving time for yourself. Here are a few examples:

Example 1: What is your time worth?

In this example, we will just look at a specific job. We will not be exploring what you have on your plate, whether you have five more jobs or no more jobs.

In our example job we will say that you bid it out for $550.00 and that it will run you $150.00 to dump everything quickly. That's a nice profit of $400.00 for you. Who would complain about having another $400.00 to spend?

Now, we will say that it will take you roughly four hours on your own to do this job by yourself and then maybe two hours to do it with a helper.

Let's say that you pay the helper $25.00 per hour. That means that instead of walking away with the entire $400.00 you would only be walking away with $350.00. Why would you do this? Well, let me ask you something: What is your time worth? If you did this job without a helper you would be making $100.00 per hour, which isn't bad. However, in the second scenario you would be making $350.00 in only two hours, therefore you would be earning $175.00 hour! And the helper will not feel at all exploited if you give them $25.00 per hour.

Even if you paid them $40.00 per hour you would walk away with $160.00 per hour. For $40.00 per hour you will have no trouble finding people to help you. It probably won't be hard finding people to help you for $25.00 per hour either, especially high school kids.

How To Make Money Doing Junk Removal

The first time you do a job and realize that you made $150.00 per hour or more on a job like that your head will be in the clouds. Trust me, it is a nice feeling, especially since you didn't have to spend several years of your life and a quarter million dollars at Harvard to do it.

Example 2: Flea Market

You may or may not be interested in getting up at 0-Dark-Early (3:30AM) to bring your stuff to a summer flea market, but I was. I actually made it four times out of maybe a dozen attempts. Getting up at that hour is a little rugged.

In my case it was a no-brainer. I lived less than five miles from one of the biggest flea markets in Connecticut, the Elephant's Trunk. For only $40.00 to get in (and several weeks subtracted from my life for getting up so early...) I had a tremendous venue for selling off stuff that I would have had to pay to get rid of.

Why do I mention all of this right here in this section? There are several reasons. First of all, you really need to have a helper at a flea market. This is because you will want food and you will need to use the restroom at some point. Even if you are some really athletic six-foot-plus German health nut, you will need to use the facilities at some point, don't kid yourself. You don't want to leave your stuff unattended. If you do, it becomes like the 'FREE' sign.

Note: make friends right away with the people next to you on either side. If there is an emergency, they will usually look out for you and your stuff, but remember, they will need to focus their attention on customers first, above all else.

That point also holds true with your own spot. Often times you will need a helper just because as you are closing a sale with one individual, your helper can be there to assist other customers, etc. You'd be surprised how often this happens.

Here is a quick story about what happened one day when I had my helper with me. We had this bolt of linen. It was really nice and was

85

three feet wide and it was really long. I think we figured that it was between eighty and a hundred feet long. You totally could have used it to escape from Riker's. At least until the swimming part kicked in…

Some guy was interested in the bolt of linen. Now, you need to understand some of the logistics of the flea market. There are the typical flea market goers that go there just to go there every once in a while, while there are others who frequent the flea markets in search of 'deals' where they know that they can turn a profit. These are usually people own some kind of store in a city or they know one or more folks that own high end boutiques of one kind or another.

BTW, this shouldn't shock you. Flea market pro's make money all the time, because they know what certain things are worth.

Anyway, there was this guy that stopped by early in the day. He was wearing a large hat, so I'll just call him Large Hat Guy. He asked how much the bolt of linen was and I couldn't believe what next boldly came out of my helper's mouth: "That bolt is one hundred dollars!"

Well, Large Hat Guy said that he'd think about it, and then he was gone.

At first I didn't know whether or not to be angry or happy with my helper. I remember saying things to her like, "If he comes back tell him we'll take eighty dollars." A second after that I said, "We'll take sixty, but not a penny less."

What neither of us understood was that this was all part of the flea market game. Large Hat Guy was probably a frequent flyer over at the flea market and probably knew that we were not since we did not look familiar to him. His strategy was most likely to come back and shake us down when the market cooled down, however I was surprised at what took place a few hours later. Large Hat Guy whipped out a fresh crisp Benjamin, handed it over to my lovely assistant and then said, "What's a hundred dollars really worth?"

Well, to me it was worth far more that the world's longest and nicest painting tarp, so I was happy. My helper received a huge bonus that day, and I can tell you that she was happy. Large Hat Guy was also happy, me knowing full well that he probably flipped the linen bolt for much more money, but I don't care. I got rid of it, and for way more than I was hoping for. Having the right helper made it happen because when it came right down to it she was adamant with her pricing, and it paid off. I probably had way too much on my mind to be that type of person with Large Hat Guy. Having the right helper at a flea market will help you preserve some of your own mental energy.

BTW, a few quick notes: By 10:30 start slashing your prices if stuff hasn't sold. You don't want to reload the truck if you can help it. Despite how long the flea market stays open, the most business is done by 11:30. By noon you should be packing up.

Pennywise and *Time* Foolish?

Sometimes we can try to squeeze every last dime out of a job. While this is generally not a bad thing, it can blind us in some cases. There are times where the extra couple of dimes of profit can rob us of much more desirable minutes/hours of time or even less measurable chunks of our happiness.

Example 1: Dump and Run!

Let's say that you can dump everything at one place for the typical fees, but that you could shave a few dollars off of the total if you make another stop or two.

The Trash Bags

Let's look at this: Maybe you could save $10.00 by not having to pay to dump a few large contractor bags of stuff since you could just as well dump them out in your own trash in five days when the trash comes. Question: Where will you put the trash in the meantime? If it's

Dave Merton

not in the way, go for it, save the $10.00. Will the wife scream? Then pay the $10.00 and be rid of them.

Also, will dumping them in the normal trash involve having to temporarily load them into your personal vehicle, like a newer car? Ooh! Don't do it. Even if you make an extra trip to drop them at the house with your junk truck before switching vehicles, is it really worth spending another fifteen to twenty minutes, plus gas, to save $10.00? No, not really.

The Clothing

This is a similar scenario. Perhaps you have two contractor bags full of halfway decent clothing. I would usually eat the $10.00 as opposed making a separate trip to some place like Good Will, etc since it is not a quick process. It would've taken me another forty five minutes to drop off the clothing like that. I'd like to think that my time is worth much more than $13.33 per hour. Now, If I am going to be heading that way anyway, then it might make more sense to visit Good Will.

I do have an exception to this rule. If you are dropping off clothing for a more *altruistic* reason, then by all means do so. There is a thrift store in my town that has been around for many years. It is operated by several older retired women. They all are volunteers. The business is a nonprofit. All the proceeds, after expenses, go toward wonderful things like scholarships for local high school seniors, etc. Because of this I didn't mind going out of my way as much.

Example 2: Money in the Mattress?

This is another great example of when the temptation to squeeze out every last penny can make you possibly regret it.

It would cost me $20.00 to dump an extra large mattress. I'd pay the $20.00, done, problem solved. Every once in a while I would think to myself how I could save all the expenditure by taking the mattress apart and piecemeal it. (Most of what I am saying here is also true for sofas and large chairs.)

There are only three parts to a box spring: Wood, metal and fabric material. Once it is all separated out you can bag up the fabric material, recycle or scrap the metal and then burn the wood as it is unfinished.

Now, all this being said, it is not fun to take apart a mattress; it takes a good half hour. (Your first may take longer.) Ask yourself: Is it really worth it to spend a brutal half hour or more to net $20.00? The answer should be a resounding 'No'.

I guess you could pay some kid $10.00 per hour to do it for you, but it still doesn't really move mountains for you in the way of finance, and you will end up 'burning' a potential helper for the important jobs.

The only time where it might make sense when you are breaking it down for strictly altruistic purposes, like in an effort to save the environment from having yet another mattress sitting in a landfill. In that case, then I totally support your efforts.

Getting Rid of Junk *Cheaply*

In this section it will sound like I am contradicting everything in the section *Getting Rid of Junk Quickly*, but I am not. Every situation is different and you alone will need to make the judgment call on which way to swing each time. My goal is to help aid you in these decisions and to try and provide you with some helpful food for thought. This will hopefully assist you in weighing the pro's and con's.

There is one basic section for this called Overall Cost. Let's look at it now.

Overall Cost

Overall cost means simply that: Dumping the most junk for the least dollars. Now my least favorite place to dump was the transfer station, but it was a necessary evil, since dollar for dollar it was the least

expensive option. The only thing is that it is not always the most practical option. In order for the transfer station to work for you, you need to have a decent sized box truck that is fully loaded with 'dumpable' stuff.

Here was my order of preference to get rid of junk, assuming that the logistics of the situation warranted me to make use of those options in a timely manner:

1. Sell the stuff and make money – of course
2. Give it away via 'FREE' sign
3. Give to Good Will or thrift store
4. Toss out on trash day - very inexpensive, but limited volume
5. Bring to recycling – cost more than transfer station, but more convenient
6. Transfer Station – Most work to dump, least cost by far

So, according to this list, if there is not enough junk to merit a trip to the transfer station in your immediate future, then I would have sold what I could, then have given away what I could, then thrown out as much as I could in the trash and then finally I would have brought the rest to a recycling type place.

Getting Rid of Junk *Easily*

One of the core lessons in this section is to bring helpers whenever you truly need them, or also when you want the job to go much faster. The more of your own energy that you keep in reserve, the smarter that you will be as the day goes by. Having a helper or two will also save on your back, etc.

Aside from utilizing helpers, the other major aspect of getting rid of junk easily ties in with the last chapter and it has to do with thinking and planning ahead. If more than one destination has to be visited to dump your junk then it really makes sense to load the truck accordingly. Just remember FILO or first in last out. (It's similar to the concept of 'stack' for all you software folks out there.)

Managing how things are loaded onto the truck will ensure the smoothest possible experience when it comes time to unload.

One last note: Even if all items are going to the same destination, it still makes sense to pack with the unloading experience in mind. What I mean by this are thinking about things like large mattresses. While they take up a lot or room and it may seem more fun to throw them in at the very end, you can have trouble when you open the truck and it causes an avalanche. Places like recycling centers, especially when it's busy (Saturday morning), hate when people cause bottle necks on them. Therefore, pack the truck with a little bit of forethought.

Chapter 8 – Estimating Jobs

Knowing how to estimate a job is crucial to your business. I will attempt to give you some pointers on this but it is not nearly as straightforward as giving someone an estimate on painting a room or building a deck. There are many more variables that come into play. I say this not to be evasive but for the following reasons:

1. Dumping costs vary from locale to locale
2. Each job has its own dynamics
   a. distance from your home/work area
   b. difficulty levels on site (what floor, what type of stairs, etc)

Let's look at these different areas I the next section.

The Many Variables in Estimating Jobs

We will cover a few of the basic dynamics that can cause you to modify pricing of a particular job. That being said how can you tell if your pricing is where it needs to be?

If everyone hires you then you might be a tad underpriced. If you are still being profitable and you are happy with the money, then it's not an issue. However, in this case most business owners would immediately begin to slowly raise their prices until they hit their 'sweet spot'.

If instead you are getting no work, or very little then you may need to lower your prices a bit.

In an ideal world you are pretty much on track if you get four out of every five jobs that you bid. Then you should be profitable and you will have located your 'sweet spot'.

Let's spend a few minutes looking into specific areas that can affect your job pricing.

Dumping Costs Vary

In different locales there may be different options for dumping. Maybe there is a landfill that actually wants your stuff. Maybe there is nothing even remotely similar to either a dump or a transfer station in your area. Maybe your best friend owns an incinerator. (Hopefully it's not the Vince Vaughn character from *Domestic Disturbance*.)

You really need to investigate these costs before you start giving out estimates. The legwork is pretty simple when it comes to a recycling center; they usually mail out their price list once per year or you can call them. They may also post all of their prices online.

Particular Job Dynamics

This next section goes over why two reclining chairs and a sleeper sofa is not necessarily the equal of just any other two reclining chairs and a sleeper sofa.

Distance From Your Home or Work base

Imagine that you have a job to do and you will be using a typical van for the job. This job is a typical average size job that has a sleeper sofa, two recliners and then several boxes of miscellaneous junk. It would all fit right into a box truck, but for this example, we are using a van. It is a two trip job. You just can't possibly get everything into the van for a single trip, not happening.

Now, let's suppose that the job is a typical $250.00 job.

If the job was right in your town (which it really should be, most of the time) and maybe ten minutes away then you can be in and out in less than two hours from getting the truck, doing the job, dumping the stuff and then parking the truck. The dumping cost would be maybe $40.00

- $60.00 depending on what was in the boxes. You probably could even get the customer to help you move the couch.

Now, let's say that instead this job was two towns away and the trip was thirty five minutes each way. You are now looking at an additional 100 minutes of travel and extra gas. Now, of course it is not the customer's 'fault' that you live where you do, but is it really your fault that they live where they do? The price to dump should remain the same, but your hourly rate would go way down.

In this example, let's say that the overall profit was $200.00. For the in-town job, $200.00 for two hours is pretty decent. For the far-away job you would be earning $200.00 for three hours and forty minutes, which translates to only $58.82 per hour. That's kind of low for this business. I mean, not many people make that even close to $58.82 per hour in their normal job, but they also get to work forty hours a week and they probably get health benefits.

Maybe you are still okay with walking away with the $200.00; after all, the extra time is just driving. However, what could you do differently? You could try to come in a little higher initially and then lower the bid as you need to.

If you wanted to 'split the difference' hour wise from the $58.82 and the $100.00 per hour, then you could simply raise the total job price by $70.00 (new price = $320.00) and then you would clear roughly $80.00 per hour. If instead you raised it by a full $140.00 (new price = $390.00) then you would clear $100.00 per hour, but it is highly unlikely that you would get the job. This is unless the customer is desperate and has nowhere else to turn.

Also, how did you get a job two towns away? Were you advertising in that area intentionally or was it through a realtor? If it was through a realtor, give the customer the best price that you can live with, but intimate to the realtor that you took a beating for their sake. This will ensure you of a slow but steady stream of repeat business.

Never burn a relationship with a realtor. They are a great source of work and it's all free. You just walk in the office, tell them what you do, hand out some cards and then leave. If there are four or more agents at once that can actually hear what you are saying you will inevitably hear someone say either, "I could have just used you on a house I just sold" or even better, "I might need you very soon on a house that is currently under contract."

The work from realtors will not make you wealthy by itself, or right away, but the acquisition cost is zero, other than a few business cards.

Difficulty Level – Job Site Logistics

In discussing why a couch is not always a couch I can remember moving a sleeper down a spiral staircase with the help of my brother. I think they built the house around this thing, because there is just no way that they got it on any more easily. At least we were going down the stairs. The customer was hilariously coming right behind us with spackle to hide the big long dent that we were putting into the sheetrock.

That job wound up costing more, even after I quoted her a decent price. She totally understood.

Other logistic issues are heavy items that may need to come out of a basement. Basement steps that go directly outside are sometimes very steep and the space is very tight.

Sometimes you need to move items across a long stretch of lawn. This may not seem like a huge deal unless you are moving something on a hand truck over wet grass.

Lastly on this subject, when you are doing a full cleanout of a house, remember that the stuff that is a few flights up is going to take longer than you think, and it is going to wear out whoever is doing the moving.

The perfect scenario logistics-wise is when the customer moves everything out into the garage for you and all you have to do is pull up with the truck. That happens once every fifty jobs maybe.

Example Bids

I am just going to spend a few minutes giving a few example bids. You will quickly learn how to adjust this information for the dynamics of your own area.

Example 1 – The 'Typical Job'

This example has been stated before but it bears repeating, since it will be in the neighborhood of your 'average' removal job.

Let's say that the customer has a sofa, a few easy chairs and then lots of eclectic crap in bags and boxes, but certainly no more than what you could easily get rid of via a free sign and then tossing the remainder out in one pickup from the trash guys. For this I would come in at $250.00. I've done jobs like this for as little as $180.00, but I would rather have the $250.00.

What if it is similar to this job, but along with a refrigerator? Add another $150.00 to $200.00.

Higher prices are more justifiable too when you have big clunky stuff like furniture since a homeowner has no real easy way to get rid of it on their own, unless they own a pickup, etc.

Example 2 – The 'Small Job'

Let's say that the job is for an appliance, like a dryer. I would normally charge $30.00 for an appliance like that. However, I also have a minimum job cost which was $50.00. I also ran an ad for $20.00 off and the offer was also on my business card, so I knew that the $20.00

off was going to come up. Because of this I would mention at the beginning that the $20.00 off cannot go below the minimum fee of $50.00. (Otherwise you are back to $30.00, which means that you are one notch over being a volunteer.)

Therefore I would tell them that it would be $50.00 as a minimum, but if they had another few things that totaled up to $70.00, then with the $20.00 off it will still end up costing them $50.00 total. They were usually okay with this and not every time would they give me more stuff to take, but sometimes they would, even if it was a few bags of trash.

In conclusion, once you figure out what is best for your area you will be able to make out well and still stomp the prices of some of the big franchise junk removal companies. They have monstrous overhead, you won't.

Specific Items

I don't always use these individual prices when I am bidding out a job; that would be too exacting. Instead, I use this list as a mental assist for when the customer asks me if I can add a few items after I am already on site and doing the work. The after-the-fact request for stuff like cans still filled with liquid paint is a great example of this. That's why I have the $10.00 per can price. They either keep the cans or they pay me the $10.00.

Below I am going to touch on some of the more popular items that seem to get added in after the fact. The list of frequent flyers is this:

1. Carpeting
2. Couches - Um, so how did they miss this the first time around?
3. Mattresses
4. Paint Cans
5. Washers/Dryers
6. Easy Chairs

Let's look at these items one by one below.

Carpeting

Old rolled carpeting is always a pain to load and then to get rid of simply because it is heavy and takes up space. If someone wants me to take it from them after I am on a job then I always charge a lot of money. If they ask why I mention how recycling centers charge me an arm and a leg because rolled up carpet takes up a lot of space in a dumpster, especially if it is not placed on the bottom.

When it comes to carpeting, especially after the fact, I am ruthless.

You also need to ask whether the carpet will require a helper or even an additional trip.

If the carpet will be impossible to load when you are done you can look the customer in the eye and say, "If only you had mentioned this to me when the truck was empty."

If I can take it with ne then I will charge at least double what they will charge me to dump it.

If I have to make a second trip and they are somewhat local it might be as high as $10.00.

Couches

So how did they not think about the couch all this time? It happens, believe me. This is also similar in spirit to the great carpet epidemic that we were just vaccinated from. Couches always need to go in first. If they happen to ask after the fact then here is a rule of thumb:

If you have room on the truck right then and there **_AND_**...
If they help you load it **_AND_**...
If it takes no more than five extra minutes,   *THEN*...

Charge them $50.00 for a regular sofa and $60.00 for a sleeper.

If it won't fit or they cannot assist you then simply say no, and offer to come back on another day for $120.00

Mattresses

This is based on how much it will cost you to dump, but if you need to price a mattress after the fact then use $30.00 as a starting point. My reasoning is that recycling centers hate them because they take up lots of space in dumpsters even though they are not ultra heavy.

Paint Cans

Any after-the-fact paint cans, with liquid paint (even one inch's worth) are $10.00 to the customer. I don't care if it is a smaller sized paint can.

If they hem and haw tell them it is because there is no real easy way to get rid of them.

Washers/Dryers

I usually tell folks that it is $30.00 per unit. Again, this is if they offer to help you load them and if they will fit on the current load and if they were smart enough to say something before the truck was loaded up. Otherwise, if another trip is merited, then you will have to figure out what it will be worth to you.

Easy Chairs

This is the same deal as the washers and dryers. Charge an extra $30.00 per easy chair. Also, it is less of an issue if they are loaded on the bottom since most easy chairs are light weight, except for recliners.

Lessons Learned

There are very few things that I have regretted when it came to my estimating. I only really underestimated four jobs out of maybe hundreds.

The all had one thing in common, they were all basement cleanouts. Three of the four were businesses that were being sold and the current owner had hired me to do the work. I will cover this in more detail in the section following: *Jobs to Avoid*.

Jobs to Avoid

There is really maybe one overall junk job type that I would say to be careful about. That type is the basement cleanout of existing mom & pop type businesses. Business owners must deal with their mess of eclectic accumulated crap when they wish to sell their business to others. They knew the day would eventually come, but the urgency is just never there until the business is under contract to be sold. Then comes the onerous task of paying someone lots of cash to move lots of junk. This is unavoidable on their part.

You actually may be wise to turn these jobs down however. Why would I say this? Because they have been accumulating junk for as long as they have owned the business. That means that there is a lot of stuff, lots of heavy, hideous stuff; and all of this stuff usually has to come up at least one full flight of stairs.

These jobs were usually harder for me to bid for a few reasons. The first one is that they are huge in comparison to the typical jobs that I usually did. This means that there would be more of a tendency to unintentionally under bid them.

Dave Merton

What made matters worse in all three of the business basement cleanouts that I did was that you just can't visualize everything that you are looking at, even though it is one monster basement, simply because everything is sectioned off and there are usually lots of shelves and partitions. This fact alone has the tendency to make you less mindful of the sheer volume of stuff you are bidding on, even if you just looked at it. I believe it is a psychological factor as opposed to a me-being-completely-stupid factor.

Lastly, you are bound to run into items that you have never moved before, since it is not residential, and this will cause you unpredictable issues. For example, in one case there were lots and lots of heavy duty steel shelves. We had to take them apart and this takes *so much* time, especially when the screw heads are all stripped.

On another job there was a lot of glass from old glass shelving. Glass is very heavy, especially when it is three quarters of an inch thick. This created both physical exertion issues as well as dumping issues. I was able to give away a few pieces, but it just stretched out the job and ate into the profits.

Chapter 9 - Handling Difficult Questions

There are times when customers will ask you questions that can put you on the spot. You really need to be prepared ahead of time as to how you will handle these questions. There are three that I want to specifically address:

1. Can you give me a price over the phone?
2. What do you do with all this stuff?
3. How do you get rid of this stuff?

The second and third questions sound like they are the same. They can be, but not always and you really need to be discerning. I will address all three of these questions, along with appropriate responses below.

Can You Give Me A Price Over The Phone

Although this commandment has been covered in a previous chapter, it is worth repeating:

NEVER GIVE OUT PRICES OVER THE PHONE.

Why not? This is like asking how much it will cost to paint a house, without seeing it. You just have no idea what will be involved.

What can you say?

"I can't give out a price over the phone. I really need to see the job in person."

If they keep asking, just keep repeating this. If you need to add more information them you could add:

"I really need to see what will be involved in removing the items."

Dave Merton

What Do You Do With All This Stuff?

This question can be touchy. This is sometimes asked by people who may think that you are going to try and profit from their stuff.

Ultimately if life had a reset button, whereby you could give a sarcastic answer, but then hit a reset button and then give them a straight answer, the sarcastic answer might be something like:

"Why do you care what I do with it? Did you just get finished listening to Alice's Restaurant for the 200th time?"

When I answer this question, I am always truthful, however not necessarily specific. This is partly because I may not yet have decided on which avenue of disposal will work out the best for the stuff that I am dumping.

I usually mention that there are several different avenues that I use to dispose of items and that it is a constant challenge to be able to organize and consolidate items so that I can most effectively dispose of all types of items in the most efficient ways both time-wise and cost-wise. (Practice saying that so that you sound like a teacher who has had to explain the same thing a million times.)

It may also be worth mentioning some of the different avenues of disposal to the customer, like the transfer station, the recycling center, the scrap yard. During these conversations it may not necessarily be as advisable to also mention other avenues like flea markets, eBay and the Bargain News. (Didn't some sales guru say to 'Keep it simple'?)

How Do You Get Rid Of This Stuff?

This question can also be touchy. The motive may be exactly the same as the last question; however it could also mean more. What the customer may want to know is where you might be bringing certain items that are not good for the environment, like tires, paint and Freon based appliances.

This is where you need to be discerning. If you think that they might be a little skittish about what you do with their unwanted stuff then you need to assure the customer that you follow all the rules and only dispose of things in the proper and legal way.

Dave Merton

Chapter 10 - The 10 Commandments

This section is information packed. It both revisits and expands on the lessons main lessons spread throughout this book. Here you will find the most important ideas consolidated into a single powerful chapter.

Commandment # 1 - Acquire Junk Jobs <u>quickly</u>, <u>easily</u> and <u>cheaply</u>!

This commandment is really the core commandment of the junk removal business. Everything else is a detail.

You need to have a steady stream of people calling you on the phone. Initially you will need to advertise in a newspaper type of vehicle. I do *not* recommend advertising in the yellow pages. The reason for this is that the yellow page ads are set up topically: Dentists are under the term "Dentist" and plumbers are under the term "Plumber". (Amazingly, I just randomly picked two of the grossest occupations on the planet. That's interesting.) The issue that we might not see right away is this: Folks that look in the yellow pages for dentists or plumbers already know that there are dentists and plumbers in the yellow pages. Most people do not consider junk removal to be a specific type of business. As a matter of fact, when you look under the term "Junk" in the yellow pages you see ads for people who will tow away your junk cars. Stick with either newspapers or 'Pennysaver' type publications.

As time goes on you will start to get more and more calls from people that you've already either done work for or people that are referrals from other people that you've done work for. In a lot of cases these people will be realtors.

In the meantime you will need to determine which periodicals will give you the most bang for the buck per advertising dollar. Commandment # 4 talks about this particular subject in more detail.

Once a printed paper publication has your ad electronically they can easily keep re-running it for you. This makes the process <u>easy</u>.

If the periodical is also weekly then you will get results more <u>quickly</u>. (I wouldn't invest in a daily publication as they tend to cost a lot more and people tend to read the ads a lot less. The proof is this: How often do you read the entire newspaper? Every day? I didn't think so.

Note: Weekly publications that are delivered/available on Thursday or Friday are the best bets, because people will be much more likely to look them over on a Saturday morning. Saturday morning is the busiest time for getting junk job phone calls.

This is how it worked for me when I was advertising (or selling):

1. <u>Housatonic Weekender</u> – Delivered to the home on Friday
2. <u>Yankee Pennysaver</u> - Delivered to the home on Thursday
3. <u>The Bargain News</u> – Available on Thursday at the news stand for a fee.

The idea of having a classified ad publication come out towards the end of the week is not a new idea, nor is it just my idea. In the junk removal business it is everything.

Once you determine the true cost of a phone call per dollar for each type of advertising vehicle, then you can determine which options are the <u>cheapest</u> and most effective for you.

Commandment # 2 - Do Junk Jobs <u>quickly</u> and <u>easily</u>!

This is the second most import commandment: to do the junk jobs quickly and easily. In order to follow this commandment you will need to look at the big picture. Besides, when it comes to work, who doesn't want everything to be quick and easy?

How To Make Money Doing Junk Removal

To make it simple to understand, just remember to always ask yourself the following three questions:

1. How many steps?
2. How many trips?
3. How many workers?

By answering these questions for each job you can you can learn how to plan and streamline the tasks that you will need to perform. Following below are more details and examples for each of these questions.

How many steps?

If you've done any kind of construction work or factory work you will immediately know what I am going to say next. Every step that you save yourself will save you time and energy over the long haul, especially when this step (or steps) are for repetitive tasks.

Imagine a factory where a worker needs to perform the same task every thirty seconds on some type of machine, perhaps a drill press. If this individual was able to somehow shave off some time in each thirty second operation, without sacrificing safety or quality, the resulting productivity could be enormous.

If this time savings was even a mere two seconds per operation it would allow the person to perform between eight and nine more operations per hour, from 120 operations to 128.6 operations. That is a 7% increase in productivity, although when you are thinking about drone work lie in a factory it is hard to get excited about the two second savings. This can be especially true if you are not the owner of the company or do not benefit directly in some way from the higher productivity, whether it be via higher compensation and/or higher recognition.

Now imagine a roofing contractor putting a new roof on your house. This example is a little easier to get excited about, if you visualize

yourself as the helper. The boss appoints you as the gopher. You get to carry all the eighty pound bundles of asphalt shingles up onto the roof. All of a sudden you seem to notice just how far the pallet of shingle bundles is from the ladder that you will be climbing. If only the person dumping the pallet had been a little smarter about it, you might conclude.

Now in a case like this, would it be possible to load several bundles into the back of a pickup and then back the pickup once to a spot right next to the ladder? Wouldn't that make more sense than walking back and forth dozens of times? Yes, it would make more sense, because instead of just 'doing the work' like a brainless automaton, you asked yourself 'how many steps'?

This type of thinking can be important especially with the really big jobs. Just moving a vehicle 10 feet closer to a door can make a huge difference in time if there will be dozens, or possibly hundreds, of trips to the truck back and forth. In addition to the actually linear footage are the other considerations like people running out of energy quicker, since carrying stuff up and down stairs many times can be quite draining physically and mentally.

Every step counts, especially for each time that you need to count it!

The next questions addresses a similar mentality but with larger scope.

How many trips?

Most of the junk jobs that I've done have been in my town or one town over. I rarely would venture more than three towns away, partly due to the fact that I focused my advertising locally.

That being said, if I lived two blocks from a junk job and the recycling center where I was going to get rid of most of the stuff was just another mile away, then whether I was to make a single trip or multiple trips on a big job is really that not relevant.

However, if the situation was a big triangle, say for example my base of operations was in one town, the job was in another town, fifteen miles away and then finally the place where I was dumping was in a third town another fifteen or so miles from either of the first two locations, then all of a sudden I would need to be a lot more careful with how many trips I was going to take. Time is money, and box trucks are not known for getting extremely high gas mileage. In a case like that an entire extra round trip could easily chew up an hour and a half to two hours of time.

Always think in terms of minimizing the amount of trips that you will need to make, unless there are really good reasons, not discussed here, that make it more feasible to break things down into multiple trips.

How many workers?

When you bring a help things can be easier. This is especially true if you need to lift something heavy or clumsy, however it is still better in some cases if you are not moving heavy stuff. There may just be a lot of stuff.

I've done many jobs completely on my own, without having a helper. This is because for many jobs it may not be feasible to pay for a helper. You would just be paying for company. However in some cases, having a helper can make the job go faster and more easily and aside from overall profit, you will actually feel better.

I've done jobs where instead of profiting $400.00 and working for maybe half the day, I would get someone else to assist, and so it would only take me half the time. The helper would not be getting half the money of course. They might be getting $20 an hour. Let's just say that you give them even more, we'll say $50.00 total for the two hours. Instead of working for a half day and making $400.00 you only made $350.00 for working two hours. I'm still happier with the $350.00 for working two hours. Why? Three reasons:

1. The job takes half the time, just two hours.

2. The hourly rate went from $100.00 an hour to $175.00 an hour!
3. The worker will be more than happy, thus enticing them to say yes the next time they are needed for a job.

There are times when you will really want to trade a few dollars in profit for the very important quality of life aspect. This means that it may be advantageous to bring a helper on some of those larger 'one person' jobs to speed things along and get you home sooner.

Commandment # 3 - Unload Junk <u>quickly</u>, <u>easily</u> and <u>cheaply</u>!

This is the next most important of the commandments, however it is the one that you may need to spend the most time thinking about, as this portion of the business tends to be more 'fluid', meaning that situations, conditions and scenarios can change every day. This information was already covered extensively in Chapters 7 and Chapter 8 and will be repeated here. One day you may load the truck one way, whereas the next day you may approach it differently, because other circumstances have changed.

The next portion of this chapter will be broken down into specific sections:

1. Unload junk *quickly*...
2. Unload junk *cheaply*...
3. Unload junk *easily*...

In some cases it may sound like the specific information in one of the following sections completely contradicts the information in another section. The shocking truth is that it may. This is not done in an effort to be confusing. It is done more to present this information in a in a 'checks and balances' way.

All of the advice is true at one time or another, but you will have to decide what works the best for you in each specific situation.

Each of these items will be described in more detail below.

Unload junk *quickly*...

In this section we were told that sometimes you will want to pay a few extra dollars, in either labor or removal costs, if it will save you a few hours of your time.

Time is money.

We went into specific details in Chapter 8 under the two sections *Do You Need Help?* and *Pennywise and time foolish?*

The lessons learned here were to get help when it makes sense to have a helper and then also to avoid trying to squeeze every last dime out of a job if it causes you to spend undo time and heartache.

Unload junk *cheaply*...

The ideas presented on this topic were primarily based on lowering the overall removal costs. Basically we were admonished to "Dump the most junk for the least dollars."

Unload junk *easily*...

This idea was discussed in various parts of the book and specifically in Chapter 8. The two main things to remember here are:

1. Get help when you need it
2. Plan ahead when loading the truck

Just those two ideas will make your life much easier.

Dave Merton

Commandment # 4 - Think big, pay small!

When it comes to purchasing a vehicle for junk removal, you really want to spend the least amount of cash for the biggest reliable vehicle that you can get your hands on. I would highly suggest looking over any of the free printed publications that may be available in your area. Usually these periodicals will be rack filled at several locations in your area, or they may be available even at a news stand for a nominal price.

One of my favorite periodicals for purchasing used vehicles in Connecticut is called The Bargain News. I have bought and sold tons of stuff through this publication. I was able to purchase both a used Ford van for $900 and then a Chevy box truck for only $700.

Needless to say, both were less than pretty, but they worked, both ran. When it comes to junk removal, the look of the vehicle is not an issue, it is how much you can fit.

You want to find something that runs.

Now, I am not a mechanic, so I will not be giving out mechanical advice; however, used vehicles are not new. Therefore, when I was shopping vehicles I made a list of the absolute most important things that I needed to have working. At the very least, any vehicle that I bought (for junk removal) would have to have all of the following things true:

1. Must be secure/lockable.
2. Emergency break must work (if you park on a hill). *
3. Make sure that the vehicle has reverse. **
4. Make sure that all lights and blinkers work. ***
5. Wipers need to work.
6. Mirrors need to be adjustable so that you can see when backing up. ****
7. Make absolutely sure that the breaks work. *****

* You really do not want to park a huge junk truck, possibly loaded with junk, on a steep hill ever really, so if your plan is to park it on a hill every night, don't. Find a nice flat parking area.

** Believe it or not, some folks never check to see if a vehicle has reverse. If you pull in somewhere and then cannot get back out, you may have serious issues.

*** This is a whole lot easier if you bring a friend.

**** Box trucks never have a view from the rear view mirror, because there is no line of site. Even a van with windows can have the rear view mirror view blocked when it is loaded with stuff.

***** Even if a truck stops okay when you are test driving it, remember that it will take longer to stop when it is loaded down with stuff. When you test drive the truck it will be empty.

Commandment # 5 - Think like you're playing Tetris → Stack Nice!

When you are loading a vehicle, don't assume that everything will fit perfectly just because you want it to.

In an effort to avoid making more than the necessary amount of trips to a pickup site (for most jobs it is only one) you need to know how to best load your vehicle.

Note: The advice here will need to be tempered with the advice also found in the next section, Commandment # 6.

There are some items that should always be placed on the floor of a vehicle, like paint cans with wet paint. You should never stack really heavy stuff on top of them either, like a dresser with really skinny legs.

Dave Merton

Certain things are really difficult to pack on a truck with everything else, like old carpeting. BTW, rolled up carpeting is wicked heavy. There are two reasons why carpet is a pain to load onto a vehicle:

1. Long and cumbersome
2. Comes at end of job

We will discuss these two items briefly.

Long and Cumbersome

Rolled up carpet, which is heavy as can be should ideally be laid flat on the floor of the vehicle. This way it is not sitting on the top of a heap, crushing everything else and waiting to fall over on top of you when you are unloading it. Sometimes the carpet cannot be laid perfectly flat and square since the length of carpet may be longer than the length of the vehicle. Then it becomes a geometry challenge where you need to do something diagonal with it. Two words: Carpet Knife. BTW, no matter how well you plan, carpet will always take up more space on your vehicle than you think. Always. Charge a lot more to remove it than you think that you should.

Having said all this, the ideal time to load the carpet would be at the beginning of the job, right? Yes, but, that is seldom the case. Read on...

Comes at End of Job

The conundrum of carting kilos of carpeting is that it tends to be one of the last things emancipated from the house. This is because sometimes it is an afterthought and the customer asks at the last minute. In other situations it is unavoidable because everything else that you are taking is sitting on top of the carpet.

If you are going to be removing carpet, you need to organize things so that it can go on first, without you having to move everything twice.

You could make the customer have it rolled and ready before you come as a term of the agreement with them.

Commandment # 6 - When making multiple trips, plan with the destination in mind before planning with the packing of the vehicle in mind.

As much as you can manage this, try to pack the van or truck in the reverse order of how you will be dumping things later. This is key, because you want to spend as little time as possible getting rid of stuff. Now, you can't do this perfectly all the time, but the more that you do this the happier you will be.

Here is a quick example. Let's say that you will be loading a bunch of stuff from a garage and a shed that is being emptied. There may be some metal items that you will simply be recycling, some scrap and then the majority of the load will be stuff that you haven't decided what to do with yet. Most of the stuff will be staying in the truck overnight.

Question 1: Are you going to be anywhere near the scrap yard? Will you have anywhere near enough scrap on the truck to make the trip worth it? Do you have the time today? If the answer to all of these things is yes, then put the scrap in last, to unload it first.

Question 2: Are you going to be passing by the recycling center after this job? If so, pack the recyclable items last so that they can be unloaded first.

How to load the vehicle, and in what order is really just common sense. Think about where you will be going first, etc, to avoid moving things around anymore than you really need to. Once again, sometimes you simply cannot avoid having to move different types of junk around a few times, but you need to minimize this as often as humanly possible.

Dave Merton

Commandment # 7 - ALWAYS USE AN APPLIANCE DOLLY WHEN MOVING AN APPLIANCE!

An appliance dolly has two things going for it that a typical hand truck does not:

1. Rear wheels
2. Nylon strap

The appliance dollies are made for appliances specifically.

Rear Wheels

The rear wheels add more support and balance when you are on level ground than you would have with just a hand truck. This is good since it is probably not good to have a refrigerator or vending machine fall backwards onto you. That wouldn't be good for you or the vending machine.

Nylon Strap

If you try to move even a smaller washing machine with just a hand truck, you can do it, but if you are not careful the washer can tip forward. That's bad. He straps on appliance dollies are really nice to have ad you can crank them tight.

Te reason why they like to tip is that the forward dimension is usually more than twice the forward dimension of the bottom plate/shelf of the hand truck. It is simple arithmetic. You can try and steady the top with one hand, but that gets tricky when you are going up or down stairs. Then you need three hands.

Commandment # 8 - ALWAYS GET ALL THE ADDITIONAL HELP THAT YOU NEED FROM

OTHER PEOPLE WHEN YOU ARE MOVING HEAVY APPLIANCES!

In a perfect world this would not need to be restated, but it does. Always get extra help if you are moving heavy appliances or other heavy items. It is never worth it to skimp on a few dollars and then to throw out your back or to rip a rotator cuff. If you have to pay someone $20.00 to go ride with you to a job and then just do 10 minutes of work, so be it. That is cheap insurance and people will line up to make an easy $20.00, believe me.

The average person can easily tip a refrigerator into a truck or van when the refrigerator is already in the driveway or on the street; however it is when the refrigerator has to be brought down a flight of stairs or pulled up a really steep set of stairs like in the case of a basement door that opens to the yard, which is very steep, that can get you into serious trouble if you try to do it single handedly.

Always get the help that you need.

Commandment # 9 - You need to get the greatest amount of calls for the least amount of dollars.

This goes back to the discussions about advertising. You really need to track where your calls are coming from as well as how many jobs you get compared to how much the add costs you. In other words, you need to locate which forms of advertising work the best for you.

Let's keep it really simple. Let's do two different situations:

Situation 1 - Let's say that after running an ad you receive 6 calls and then do 4 of those 6 jobs. We'll say that the ad cost you $90.00.

Situation 2 - Let's say that after running an ad you receive 8 calls and then do 7 of those 8 jobs. We'll say that the ad cost you $150.00.

Dave Merton

Of these two examples which would you say was better for you? We will pretend for the sake of this example that each job was the same amount of work and the same amount of profit. No two jobs are ever the same amount of work or profit, but we just want to highlight the advertising side of things.

It first of all depends on how you are determining value. Is it based on calls rec'd or jobs done? The reason why this is important to understand is that the purpose of advertising is to make the phone ring, not to get jobs.

That may seem confusing, let me explain. An advertisement can give two different people the same 10 phone calls. Person 1 may call the customer right back, set an appointment and then go see the customer the same day or the next day, while Person 2may not get back to the customer for a week. Who do you think will get more work? It would be Person 1 for sure. You can't blame the ad because of poor business practices.

In addition, two more people could wind up with the same 10 calls but then 1 person may understand how to the bid the jobs correctly whereas the person may not.

The sole purpose of advertising is to make the phone ring. It is up to you from that point forward to make the jobs happen.

Please look at the chart below:

	Situation 1	Situation 2
Ad cost	90.00	150.00
Calls	6	8
Average Call cost	15.00	18.75
Jobs	4	7
Average Job cost	22.50	21.43

How To Make Money Doing Junk Removal

This chart illustrates that if you are correctly looking at how many calls that you received (as opposed to how many jobs that you did) then Situation 1 ($15.00/call) was actually better than Situation 2 ($18.75) for actual calls received per dollar.

If instead you were just looking at how many actual jobs that you did (which is not a direct correlation to the effectiveness of an advertisement) per dollar spent then you would have misguidedly concluded that Situation 2 ($21.43/job) was slightly better than Situation 1 ($22.50/job).

Do you see why this distinction between calls received and then jobs done is important? Perfectly good calls from an advertisement can be squandered if you do not call the customer right back and/or bid the job in the right way. That is not the fault of advertising.

Therefore, technically speaking, Situation 1 outperformed Situation 2 in the way that *most* matters, which is the number of actual calls received per advertising dollar spent. That being said, both advertisements were still well within the bounds of what I would consider to be worthwhile investments for advertising purposes.

Commandment # 10 - DO NOT GIVE OUT PRICES OVER THE PHONE!

This just cannot be mentioned enough times. NEVER EVER give out prices over the phone. This is because you really need to see what you will be taking as well as what will be involved in getting the stuff from the house or barn to the vehicle.

My brother and I had to grab a couch from a house this one time and so I told the woman over the phone that it would normally be maybe $75 - $80 to get it, unless we ran into anything strange. As it turned out, the couch had to be brought down a spiral staircase and it was a sleeper sofa, so it was twice as heavy. (You would think that they built the house around this sofa. I have no idea how they were able to get it up the staircase when they first bought it.) We also scraped up the

Dave Merton

walls on the way down. The woman was very nice and appreciated what we were doing and was literally spackling right behind us as we were dinging up the wall. She wound up giving me $125.00 for our troubles, which was fair.

This woman was actually quite nice and reasonable. However, this job could have gone bad. She could have threatened to sue me for dinging up the wall, etc. She could have said that I quoted her $75 - $80 over the phone, etc. That's why it's such a bad idea to give prices over the phone. In this case it worked out, but we are talking about a couch, not a garage full of goodies.

Note: On a related note, when you are looking over stuff and giving estimates, please do this when there is decent lighting. If you happen to be in a basement for example, that is quite dark and there might be better light during the day, when sunlight comes through the basement windows, then you might be much better off looking at it during the day. I got really burnt on a job once because it was someone I knew and I looked at the job when it was dark in the basement. I charged $250.00, thinking it would take me a half day and that I would pocket $180 - $190. Well, it took me over 2 full days and my profit wound up being on $50.00, because I wasn't able to see all the stuff that was really there. (Unless of course it magically grew over night…)

Chapter 11 - What I Would Do Differently

If I went back into the junk removal business there are a few things that I think I would do differently. (BTW, I do actually think of going back into this business all the time, because it can be so fun.)

Curb Side Service

One of the things I think that I might insist on is that for jobs that are just a removal of a single item (like a refrigerator, other appliance or a monstrously heavy television set) is that the customer would be responsible for bring the item to the curb. If I had to yank it from the house, I would then tack on more money.

An example of this would be like so for a refrigerator:

Old Way:	I come and get it no matter where it is:	$150.00
New Way:	Curb side:	$150.00
	I come and get it no matter where it is:	$150.00+

The $150.00+ would be open ended, based on how much work was involved in extracting the refrigerator from its hiding place. I know of another individual who just charges $200.00 to remove a refrigerator.

Storage

Back in the day I had rented out a few storage units. This was necessary because I did not have the room to store things where I was living.

Also, storage facilities are nice because they always have dumpsters. Normally you as a renter are not supposed to put things in the dumpster. Some storage places put locks on their dumpsters because idiot renters will stick things in there that really shouldn't go in, like

Dave Merton

old air conditioners, paint cans with paint or my favorite stupid thing, mattresses that stick way over the sticker that says not to place anything above it.

However, if you ask the person running the facility for permission, and if you don't abuse the privilege, then you can sometimes get away with feeding the dumpster. Always be super nice to the person running the storage place. Think of them as a foreign diplomat. Be nice.

However, storage costs money. Ideally, a single guy with a house and a two car garage could set himself up really nicely and not have to ever need to use a storage unit.

On the other hand, if you are a guy and not single, then a really understanding wife would also do the trick. Um, if you are happily married, pretend that you never read the previous sentence. ☺

One New Idea…

I am a real fan of something called 'permaculture'. This is the idea of not only growing your own organic food, year round, but also the re-using and re-constituting of personal property so that the property does not end up in landfills.

A quick example of this is one person who is throwing out several flower pots, perhaps with potting soils and plants still in them, because they have to move, and then a second person who is going to go to Wal-Mart to buy brand new flower pots, potting soils and seeds.

Just imagine if there was a greater awareness in your local community about permaculture. As a junk removal person, you might be able to get rid of some items that could actually be useful to those that would like nothing better than to take some of your 'junk' and re-constitute it. Wood scraps can be used in gardening for stakes, etc. The possibilities are endless.

My thinking just wasn't as developed and 'green' back then as it is now. I am really interested in preserving the planet I live on and having a tiny carbon footprint.

How about you?

Chapter 12 – Funny Stories

The following sections go over a few of the funny stories about things that actually happened when I was doing junk removal. This list is by no means exhaustive, but I thought I'd mention a few varying types of funny stories.

The Free Sign!

When I used to live at my friend's house, he would begrudgingly let me put 'free' stuff out in the front yard. This was a major way of getting rid of stuff for free. (Free to them and free for me.)

The house was in a prime location on one of the busiest streets in our town. There was decent parking, so people could see the stuff, and then stop. I would always have a 'FREE' sign visible from both directions, with just the word 'FREE' in huge black letters, so that it could be seen from a mile away, possibly even from space. The whole trick, besides ample traffic, is to have the ability for people to get curious and then be able to make the two second decision to pull over, get out and take stuff.

The people driving by every day were becoming trained to keep a look out for the day's newest, freshest free stuff. My friend's house was becoming famous much more quickly than he was.

So this one day, I couldn't find my 'FREE' sign, someone must have taken it with the rest of the stuff that they took. No biggy, I'm sure that it was an honest mistake. Besides, for me it is a relatively small price to pay to have this really inexpensive junk removal service. You'd think that my customers would have at least tried this route to get rid of stuff. Maybe they weren't on busy streets.

I had to make new 'FREE' sign really quick so that I could put some stuff out front. I was in a hurry so I took a piece of 8.5x11 paper and typed out something close to the following:

Dave Merton

Okay, so I had my newly printed sign, ready to go. Just one problem, paper likes to blow away, so I had to weigh it down, or tape it to something or like hire the Travelocity Gnome to sit there and hold it

So, what to do? Necessity is the mother of invention, and, speaking about mothers, my mother will absolutely *kill* me if she ever finds out about this next decision of mine. Let's keep this one close to the vest, shall we? I looked around and saw this really nice Normal Rockwell print that my mother had given to me. It was a lovely print, but she had put it in this really nice (and heavy) wooden frame. As soon as I saw that, the FREE sign went in and Norman came out. I then had my 'heavy enough' new 'FREE' sign.

You can guess the rest. I came home hours later, and all the junk was gone. Yes! But then I noticed that so was the really nice picture frame. Doh! However, I couldn't stop laughing because the person who took the frame did actually follow the rules and they left the piece of paper, so technically they took everything (including the frame) except the actual paper sign.

I still laugh about that.

Sorry Mom.

☺

Do You Still Do This?

One thing that seems to be a constant in this business is the fact that some people will save your business card or they will cut out and save your advertisement.

In some cases, they will do this knowing that they may not need your services for several months, if not closer to a year. It could be that they have a home for sale and do not know exactly when it will sell, but they definitely know that they will need to get rid of junk.

Now, this may not be shocking, but many of the people who have done a serious junk removal business have not necessarily done it full time over many consecutive years. I actually chose to leave the business when I was offered a fulltime position at a software company.

I say this because for many potential customers the idea of doing junk removal as a lifelong business is not as legitimate or professional as someone who might be a landscaper or an attorney.

I say this, not to dissuade you from trying out this business at all, I am merely stating a fact based on my years of observation. It is human nature. Because of this perception, those customers who do clip your ad and then need to finally call you twelve to fifteen months later may actually wonder if you are still in the business. Once you get past the irony that they need your services, but can't see the legitimacy, you can have some fun with it. Here is what will inevitably happen, I kid you not... Some people who call you (after having your business card or clipped ad after a year) will say the following: *Do you still do this?*

It is pretty hilarious. They are guessing you don't, but are secretly hoping you do. See the irony?

You will get calls like this. When you hear them ask you if 'you still do this', just smile.

Dave Merton

"Wendy"

I once was asked to come give an estimate at a rather upscale home. It was quite large and had a huge yard. The yard size was a key to this story, since it makes it ten times funnier at least.

The woman, let's call her "Wendy" had told me that she was going through a divorce. I thought to myself that it was too bad about that, the home was nice, the yard was nice and 'Wendy' was very attractive, kind and maybe in her late 30's. I just couldn't understand it, but it wasn't my place to judge, after all, I was the junk guy.

She also told me that the house was being sold and that she was moving. I probably could have figured out the moving part since there was this HUGE moving van blocking off the driveway.

There were two moving guys that were loading the van and there was also a guy in slacks and dress shirt that was with the moving guys who didn't really do much of anything other than not help the other two guys. He must have been like a 'supervisor' or something.

Anyway, picture how strange it would be if 'Wendy' was helping the moving guys move stuff. She wasn't, but just think how unusual it would have looked if 'Wendy' was helping one of the moving guys carry a monster sleeper sofa out of the house while supervisor guy and the other moving guy were either eating lunch or playing cards. That would never happen in a million years. (I mean, maybe this might happen in some bizarre scene in an Adam Sandler movie but not real life.)

So anyway, I had already put almost everything onto the truck that had to go and there were just had a few more items that needed to be brought out.

'Wendy' and I had sort of hit it off over the half hour or so that I was there so she decided that she would save me a trip and help me carry out the last few items. I said that it wasn't necessary, but she insisted, so I thanked her and discussed what was left.

Now, here is where this gets ridiculously funny.

If I said that there was a vacuum cleaner, a paint can and a trash bag this wouldn't be very funny.

If I said that there was trash bag and a pillow and a cardboard box of old clothes this wouldn't be very funny.

However, what was there was a lamp and a pillow and an exercise machine. The exercise machine was a huge & heavy treadmill. You know, the kind that they kill people with at the gym. So, of course I went to grab the treadmill, it was reflex:

> A man → the heavy stuff
> A woman → the easy stuff

It was like an automatic response on my part.

But that's when 'Wendy' said, "Wait, hold on a minute. How heavy is that?" She then went over to it and tried moving off of the ground. I was trying not to chuckle. To my surprise 'Wendy' lifted the monster treadmill off of the ground and said, "I've got this!" (I so want her on my Navy Seal team.) I picked up the remaining items, the pillow and the lamp. That is to say, I man-handled the not-very-heavy lamp and the not-very-manly pillow.

Now, I thought that I was going to be embarrassed as we went outside and had to trek to the truck over her big long lawn. Why? Because she, both a lady and the customer, was carrying a huge heavy piece of equipment and I, the helpful-hired-hefty-hunk was carrying a lamp and a pillow. This was so not-right on so many levels, however it makes for a good story... Yes, it just wasn't the right thing to do, but it was what 'Wendy' had wanted. However, as we went outside, with me leading the procession, the most amazing thing happened. The moving guys stopped moving. They were just staring at us. The supervisor guy who wasn't really doing anything stopped doing even that, and he was

Dave Merton

staring at us too. It was as if they all three were thinking "How did he pull this off?" It could have been one of those scenes in a movie where one of the guys drops his mouth and his cigarette falls out as he is staring in disbelief. That's when I realized what was truly happening. They must have thought that I was "the man".

It makes for a funny story over beers, but just for the sake of humor. In real life women must always be treated with the deepest respect. Wherever 'Wendy' is today, I hope that she is doing well. She deserves it.

Dave Merton

Resources

The chapter will list helpful resources. The first section will consider valuable resources that are essentially worldwide.

The second section will be for valuable resources that are specific to the area from which I operated from, in case the reader just happens to be in the New England or Tri-State area of the US.

Global Resources

These are the global resources available to all.

eBay

For online auctions, the most popular site in the world is eBay:

www.ebay.com

I have personally sold many items via eBay, not just related to my junk removal business. Related to the junk removal business I sold everything from speakers to Electrolux vacuum cleaners.

Google

Google is the world's leading internet search engine.

www.google.com

You can use it to locate local forms of advertising, local scrap yards and local places to dump junk, like recycling centers, landfills and perhaps even areas that are aggressively looking for clean brush.

Dave Merton

Local Resources (Connecticut based)

The Bargain News

This is a paid publication that you can purchase at the news stand every Thursday in CT. It really works well. Placing an ad is free.

www.bargainnews.com

The Elephant's Trunk

This is one of the best flea markets in Connecticut and is open every Sunday from mid March to early December.

I personally used to go here in the late 70's (when I was 12/13) with my friend Chip and we would spend our hard earned cash on old Marvel comics.

I also had the opportunity to sell a lot of 'treasure' at this flea market from my junk business.

The fee is currently $50.00 for vendors and you can't beat it.

www.etflea.com/_/Home.html

The Yankee Pennysaver

This is a weekly publication that is mailed to several towns in the greater Danbury area. You can place display ads and /or classified ads.

This publication worked very well for me *and* they are still in business after 18 years despite a tricky economy. They remain in business because their publication really works well for their advertisers. This is a testament to the Yankee Penny Saver's expert leadership.

To check out the Yankee Pennysaver on line go here:

www. ctpennysaver.com

About the Author

My name is Dave Merton, I live in New Milford, CT and I'm a robust 47 years of age. I am a software engineer by trade, but in 2003 I was forced to go back into doing construction and small remodeling jobs. I was fine with that because to me, doing a remodeling job isn't really work, it's more like fun. Compared to sitting in front of a PC for ten hours, ripping a bathroom apart and re-tiling it is like playing.

As I was sitting at the kitchen table (I know this sounds like the beginning of one of those 'make 20,000,000 dollars in the next half hour' scams, but it's really true, I was in the kitchen...) I just out of the blue started wondering how much money I could make by doing junk removal. After a few minutes of pondering, and then thinking about the secondary avenues of reselling, I actually started laughing out loud.

Shortly thereafter I had an ad in the paper, was using my very not-so-pretty-cream-and-rust-colored '89 Ford Econoline to do junk jobs, and was making a TON of extra cash. It literally saved me. I soon had to obtain a box truck. I found an older beat up one in the bargain news for 1000 bucks. They guy totally didn't want it anymore it was just an eyesore. I offered him 700. He accepted. I then had my first 'fleet'.

From that point, I had to figure everything out as I went along. The situation was very rewarding in many ways. You really learn how to network, and you really know how to create a lot of win/win situations.

If you're anything like me, you'll love doing this business.

In 2005 I was offered a position at a software company which is owned by a friend of a friend. I would have been foolish not to accept the job, so I took it. I still dabbled in junk removal for a while, but eventually realized that I did not want to continue doing both.

Dave Merton

Besides, I removed most of the junk in my area, so I need to give these folks time to accumulate more junk.

I'm just biding my time…

☺

Made in United States
Orlando, FL
14 March 2024